CULTURES OF THE WORLD®

CHAD

Martha Kneib

 **Marshall Cavendish**
Benchmark

New York

PICTURE CREDITS

Cover photo: © Tom Stoddart Archive/Getty Images

AFP: 24, 27, 28, 32, 34, 47 53, 97, 108, 109, 118 • age fotostock/Kevin O'Hara: 6, 7, 15, 17, 18, 41, 48, 50, 60 • age fotostock/Targa: 3, 10, 85, 91 • ANA Press Agency: 90, 111 • Bes Stock: 44, 46, 65, 67, 71, 72, 83, 86, 88, 104, 121, 123 • Bridgeman Art Library: 20, 22 • California Newsreel: 106 • Corbis Inc.: 1, 4, 12, 13, 16, 19, 26, 30, 35, 61, 66, 68, 70, 101, 102, 116, 120 • Eye Ubiquitous/Hutchinson: 125, 127, 128 (Macus Stace) • Getty Images: 5, 25, 31, 36, 37, 40, 51, 58, 63, 64, 77, 78, 80, 92, 100, 113, 124, 129 • Lonely Planet Images : 43, 87 • Photolibrary: 57 • R. Ian Lloyd: 9 (Royalty Free) Reuters: 39, 76, 79, 89 • Still Pictures: 73, 74, 98, 110, 114, 115, 126 • Stockfood: 131 • Top Foto: 56 • www.tropix.co.uk: 8, 11, 49, 62, 112 (D. Davis); 54, 95 (R. Cansdale); 103 (V. and M. Birley)

PRECEDING PAGE

A group of Chadians dressed in colorful clothes stand under a tree.

ACKNOWLEDGMENTS

Thanks to Jean Sramek, Kelley Briles, Helbongo Dominque Malla, and Pamela Lepkowski for all their help.

Marshall Cavendish Benchmark
99 White Plains Road
Tarrytown, NY 10591
Website: www.marshallcavendish.us

Series concept and design by Times Editions
An imprint of Marshall Cavendish International (Asia) Private Limited
A member of Times Publishing Limited

Library of Congress Cataloging-in-Publication Data
Kneib, Martha.
    Chad / by Martha Kneib.—1st ed.
      p. cm.—(Cultures of the world)
    Summary: "Provides comprehensive information on the geography, history, governmental
      structure, economy, cultural diversity, peoples, religion, and culture of Chad"—Provided by
      publisher.
    Includes bibliographical references and index.
    ISBN-13: 978-0-7614-2327-0
    ISBN-10: 0-7614-2327-3
    1. Chad—Juvenile literature. I. Title. II. Series.
    DT546.422.K54 2007
    967.43—dc22   2005027079

Printed in China

7 6 5 4 3 2 1

CONTENTS

A rock formation on the Ennedi Massif mountain, near Guelta d'Archei, a canyon in Chad.

A Kreda girl balances a large bowl on her head.

INTRODUCTION

CHAD IS ONE OF THE LEAST-KNOWN countries in Africa, despite having a rich history. Chad's location at the crossroads between the Sahara desert and Central Africa has made it a land where people have passed through, met, settled, and resettled for many centuries.

The presence of a large number of ethnic groups and languages contributes to the colorful fabric of Chadian history and makes it one of the most culturally diverse lands in the world. New income in the form of oil revenue has given a boost to the economy and is providing Chad a chance to expand its social and educational programs.

Although the people of Chad have been through much turmoil in the form of droughts, wars, and diseases in the recent past, they have emerged from these trials ready to embrace a more positive future.

GEOGRAPHY

CHAD IS A LANDLOCKED COUNTRY in central Africa. It is bordered by six other countries: Libya to the north; Niger, Nigeria, and Cameroon to the west; the Central African Republic to the south; and Sudan to the east. The country stretches for 1,080 miles (1,800 km) from its northernmost point to its southernmost point. The average width of the country is 497 miles (800 km). Chad covers a total of 495,624 square miles (1,284 million square km). It is roughly three times the size of California.

Because the country is landlocked, it has no ports. Its capital, N'Djamena, is more than 683 miles (1,027 km) from the Atlantic Ocean. An eastern city, Abéché, is 1,646 miles (2,649 km) from the Red Sea, and a northern city, Faya-Largeau (sometimes referred to as Faya), is 962 miles (1,548 km) from the Mediterranean Sea.

Left: **The Faya-Largeau Oasis on the Ennedi Massif.**

Opposite: **A caravan passes by the Archai Rocks in the Chadian region of the Sahara desert.**

GEOGRAPHIC REGIONS

Chad boasts a wide variety of terrains, from deserts to tropical rain forests. It has mountains, plains, and deep basins containing interesting rock formations. This diversity has traditionally been divided into four geographical zones: Saharan, Sahelian, Sudanian, and Humid Tropical.

SAHARAN ZONE The Saharan zone in northern Chad is a desert. It receives less than 8 inches (20 cm) of rain per year. This area supports few permanent settlements due to the lack of available water sources. As with all other deserts, the land gives up its heat quickly in the evening, leading to large temperature fluctuations between day and night.

This desert region is home to Chad's highest point, a volcanic peak called Emi Koussi, which is 11,205 feet (3,415 m) above sea level. Emi Koussi peak is not only the highest point in the country, but also the highest in the Sahara desert.

The lowest point in the country, the Djourab Depression, is also in this zone. It is 535 feet (163 m) above sea level and is in the northeastern part of the country. The rugged area where Emi Koussi lies is along the Chadian-Libyan border. It is called the Tibesti Massif. A massif is an area of a mountain range independent of the rest of the range.

The Tibesti Massif is made of very old rocks separated from the other massifs to the east and the west by deep basins of younger rock. It contains areas of surface water in permanent pools, which are called *gueltas*. *Gueltas* are usually found in low points, such as ravines. This area also has seasonal watercourses. What little rainfall there is usually occurs between February and May.

The city of Faya lies within this desert zone. The town is situated at an oasis near the Tibesti Massif and is one of the largest oasis towns in the world, with a population of around 5,000. The town is surrounded

Rock formations in Tibesti, Chad.

An interesting rock formation in the Ennedi Massif, near Guelta d'Archei. These towers and spikes are the result of years of wind erosion.

by cliffs. Subterranean water makes agriculture possible near Faya where wheat, dates, and figs are grown. Faya has been known to go more than a decade without significant rainfall. Because there are no paved roads in this area, those who wish to travel to Faya must use four-wheel-drive vehicles. The distance from the capital city, N'Djamena, to Faya is 589 miles (948 km).

North of Faya are three small lakes that are famous for their colorful water. Minerals in the water produce one lake that is blue, another red, and the third purple. Several species of birds can be found there, such as the desert lark, the desert sparrow, and the trumpeter finch.

Another town in the region is Fada, which has a population of around 1,500. There are interesting rock formations around the town. The best-known geological formation is the Guelta d'Archei, a narrow red rock canyon that has been eroded over the ages into many fascinating towers and spikes. Deep in the canyon there are freshwater pools that are frequented by baboons. Fada is 683 miles (1,099 km) from the capital city.

SAHELIAN ZONE The Sahelian zone of Chad encompasses the central portion of the country and contains the capital city and Lake Chad. This zone, part of the semi-arid Sahel region of Africa, represents a transitional area between the Sahara desert to the north and the tropics to the south. Rainfall in the zone is highly irregular and is usually less than 20 inches (51 cm) per year.

The northern part of the Sahelian zone is open grassland and thornbushes, while farther south is the savannah. The eastern part of the zone rises up to the remote Ennedi Massif. The highest point of the massif is Basso Peak, which is 4,757 feet (1,450 m) above sea level.

The Sahelian zone has a varied ecosystem. The arid thicket rat, which prefers lower elevations, is found in the region, as well as two endangered native gerbils, Burton's gerbil and Lowe's gerbil, which are found at higher elevations. Both gerbil species are considered critically endangered.

Larger animals, such as a desert antelope called the addax and several species of gazelle, such as the *gazella dama*, *gazella dorcas*, and *gazella rufifons*, also live in the Sahel. These animals are considered threatened but not yet endangered. Until the 1980s the scimitar oryx was found here, but it is now considered extinct in the wild.

Other animals that live in this region are the sand fox, a wild cat, known as the caracal, the brown cape hare, the rock hyrax, and the desert hedgehog. These species are common.

Wildlife in the zone are well adapted to the dry climate in which they live. The *gazella dorcas*, for instance, can acquire all the water it needs from the plants it eats.

Desert hedgehogs, the smallest of its species, are common in the Sahel.

The marabou stork is common in arid areas of Africa, including Chad. This stork is able to survive by eating scraps, dead animals, and even garbage.

Wildebeests are a common sight in Chad's national park, Parc National de Zakouma.

SUDANIAN AND HUMID TOPICAL ZONES South of the Sahelian zone is the Sudanian zone. This region is dominated by a long dry season of six to nine months and a rainy season when up to 24 inches (61 cm) of rain falls every year.

The southern tip of Chad lies in the Humid Tropical zone, where more than 36 inches (91 cm) of rain falls every year. In this zone the rainy season lasts six to nine months, and the dry season is short. Temperatures are high year-round. These two zones are covered in savannah with stands of bushes and trees.

Wild animals are commonly found, partly due to reintroduction. Chad's game park, Parc National de Zakouma, is in the Sudanian zone. The park was opened in 1958 and it occupies 1.1 million acres (445,145 ha). During the dry season, visitors can get to see elephants, giraffes, lions, wildebeest, and many species of antelope. Due to the condition of the roads, traveling to the park, touring it, and getting back to the capital city can take six days.

Animal density in the park is higher than at many other parks in East Africa or South Africa, but park facilities and wildlife have been damaged by the country's civil war and so far the park has not been able to attract as many tourists as its creators had hoped for.

Park animals are vulnerable to villagers nearby who kill them for food, so some effort has been made to involve the villagers in running the park. Most villagers live in poverty and if they have other means of acquiring food to feed their families, such as earning money by taking care of the park, the park animals may face fewer threats.

RIVERS AND LAKES

Chad has two permanent rivers. The Chari River flows for 745 miles
(1,199 km) and is formed from the tributaries of the Gribingui, Bamingui,
Bahr Sara, and Bahr Salamat rivers. The other river is the Logone River.
This river flows for 602 miles (969 km) and is formed from the tributaries
of the Pende and M'Bere rivers. The Logone River forms part of the border
with Cameroon and merges with the Chari River near N'Djamena. These
rivers are navigable only during the rainy season.

The most important body of water that borders Chad, Niger, Nigeria,
and Cameroon is Lake Chad. This lake occupied several hundred thousand
square miles in prehistoric times when the area was much wetter. But
it has since shrunk to a fraction of its former size. Even so, it is the
seventh largest lake in the world. Ninety-five percent of the lake's water
comes from the Chari River. During the rainy season, the lake may cover
9,843 square miles (25,493 square km). During the dry season, it covers
only 3,782 square miles (9,795 square km).

Besides changing in size during the year, the lake may vary greatly from year to year. In 1870 the lake covered 10,808 square miles (27,993 square km), but it had shrunk to 4,902 square miles (12,696 square km) by 1908. The lake remained small till the end of the 1950s. After a wet period in the early 1960s, the lake regained most of its 1870 size, and by 1963 it covered 10,036 square miles (25,993 square km).

Lake Chad is very shallow; in recent centuries the lake has had a depth of less than 23 feet (7 m). Droughts during the 1970s and 1980s, however, caused the water level of the lake to drop to the point where in 1984 it was possible to walk across it. In the future, increases in water demands by the four countries that border the lake might shrink it even further.

Chad has two other lakes, Lake Fitri and Lake Iro. Lake Iro is in the southeastern region of the country in a marshy area. Lake Fitri receives its water from seasonal watercourses, called wadis, in the northern region

POLDERS

North of Lake Chad are polders. Polders are a series of dikes that connect the islands and peninsulas along the shore. Floodwater is drained into the polders, and when it evaporates in the dry season, rich soil is left behind. The Buduma and Kotoko people who maintain the polders are able to raise two and sometimes three wheat crops each year. After 10 years, the polders are flooded for three years to regenerate the soil.

Due to the irregularity of the surface area of Lake Chad, the polders are only flooded during exceptionally rainy seasons, while during droughts only those closest to the lake will have water. The polders make approximately 150,000 acres (60,703 ha) of land available for agriculture, of which about half is being used at any one time.

of the country that flow only during the rainy season. The northern part of the country has no permanent watercourses.

After the rains, the wadis are full of fish, which people catch and eat. The fish survive the dry seasons by burrowing deep in the mud and sleeping until the next time it rains. Although young men will brave the watercourses to catch fish, most people in the desert are afraid of water because flash floods are common and can without warning, easily overcome and drown anyone in the wadi's channel. Such flash floods kill many people in desert areas around the world every year.

Chad is a large country with a small, unevenly distributed population. Most Chadians live in the south near Lake Chad and the country's two rivers.

Yoa Lake, a temporary lake in the Ounianga Kebir Region on the Ennedi Massif, fills up with water after the rainy season.

Women sell food at a market in Chad's capital, N'Djamena.

PREFECTURES AND THE CAPITAL

Chad is composed of 14 prefectures, or administrative divisions. Within these 14 prefectures live more than 9 million people who belong to nearly 200 ethnic groups. Two of the main prefectures are Chari-Baguirmi and Borkou-Ennedi-Tibesti (BET).

Covering 231,735 square miles (600,191 square km), the BET prefecture makes up almost half of the entire country of Chad. It is administered from Faya. Very few people live in this prefecture, as it lies within the Sahara desert. Most of this region is extremely remote, and sandstorms constantly erase tracks and signs of truck routes. It can take up to two weeks for trucks to get from the capital city of N'Djamena to Faya.

Aouzou is a military outpost in the north of this prefecture. The area where it is located, the Aouzou Strip, was occupied by Libyan forces in 1975, as it was believed that the area held deposits of uranium. During the 1980s, Chadian forces recovered much of the area, but it was not until 1994 that an international court determined that the entire region belonged to Chad. In May 1994, the United Nations forces oversaw the withdrawal of the remaining Libyan troops.

The Chari-Baguirmi prefecture covers 32,003 square miles (82,887 square km) and has an estimated population of nearly 850,000. The population of the prefecture has doubled since the 1970s, mostly because this prefecture encompasses Chad's capital, N'Djamena.

Until September 6, 1973 N'Djamena was known as Fort Lamy. Its current name comes from a village, Am-Djamena, which was itself named after a local tree species. Its population is estimated to be between 650,000 and 800,000 people. Before 1984 conveniences such as electricity and water were either not present in the city or tightly rationed. Conditions have improved in the capital since that time.

Although N'Djamena still bears the scars of Chad's 30-year civil war, small signs of growth have appeared. The main street, Avenue du General de Gaulle, has several restaurants including a French restaurant and a Lebanese restaurant. The city has one museum, the Musée National, founded in 1963. The museum has displays documenting Chad's prehistory, paleontology, and ethnography. It also has an extensive collection of African art and is the home of the national archives.

A lack of basic services in the city remains. Many neighborhoods have taken it upon themselves to set up waste disposal services, since the city lacks an effective system of collecting and disposing refuse. Volunteers working in committees assemble donkey carts to haul trash out of the city to outlying dump sites. The committees have also built public restrooms. They originally had assistance from the UN Development Agency (UNDP) and are now raising funds for their work by selling waste containers.

The remote Bambeche region in the BET prefecture.

HISTORY

THE HISTORY OF HUMAN INHABITATION in Chad goes back to ancient times. Scientists have discovered that northern Chad was once home to one of the earliest hominids known to science.

In 2002 scientists published an article in *Nature* describing a newly discovered creature. Its remains were nicknamed Toumaï, which is a traditional name in the region for babies born before the dry season.

Toumaï was found in deposits with animals known to have lived 7 million years ago. These include elephants, three-toed horses, giraffes, monkeys, and relatives of the hippopotamus called anthracotheriids.

Modern humans have also lived in the area for quite a long time. Rock art paintings in the north of the country depict big-game animals such as antelopes in areas that are now desert. These paintings were made thousands of years ago when the area was much wetter and had an abundance of wildlife.

For thousands of years the area dried out, but it remained a place of trade and migration routes. Two thousand years ago, during the Roman Empire, caravans passed through the area with goods bound for Rome. Throughout prehistoric and recorded history, the area that is now Chad has been important for many people.

Above: **A scientist holds Toumaï's skull in the paleontology room of N'Djamena University.**

Opposite: **Prehistoric cave paintings in Marmar Tassili on Chad's Tibesti Massif.**

EARLY KINGDOMS

Around the 11th century, several ethnic groups who lived in the northern area of what is now Chad formed a kingdom under the leadership of a group called the Zaghawa. The Zaghawa were made up of many families, and it was the Sefuwa family that established themselves as the ruling family. The Sefuwa dynasty ruled for centuries and was responsible for expanding the kingdom, named Kanem-Borno, into neighboring areas. By the 12th century, the kings of Kanem controlled many of the east-west and north-south caravan routes through the desert.

In the past, a key component of Chad's economy was the slave trade. *A Sand Wind in the Desert* depicts slave traders bringing in slaves.

20

Traders brought Islam into the area and the kings of Kanem converted from their native religion. Most of the local people, however, did not convert to Islam until around the 12th and 13th centuries when the kingdom became large enough for great quantities of trade to come through. By that time, Kanem was an important route not only for trade but also for Muslim pilgrims on their way to Mecca.

In A.D. 1356 the Sefuwa lost their power and were exiled to a region called Borno. But they eventually regained their power over Kanem and founded what became known as the Kanem-Borno Empire, which lasted for 500 years.

Famines in the 17th and 18th centuries began to undermine Sefuwa control of the empire. Invasions from nomadic groups such the Tuareg and the Fulani created insecurity. Bit by bit, Kanem-Borno became smaller, and the king less powerful. In 1808 the empire's capital city was destroyed in a raid by the Fulani. The king moved the capital to a new location, but eventually the French overwhelmed the last remaining pockets of the king's power and the kingdom fell. Today all that remains of the capital of the Kanem-Borno Empire is ruins.

ALUMA

Aluma was the most celebrated king of Kanem-Borno. He reigned from 1571 to 1603. An epic poem written about him tells of his victories in 1,000 battles. Aluma employed many military techniques new to the area: soldiers mounted on camels, walled military camps, permanent sieges, armored soldiers and horses, and musketeers trained by foreign military specialists. He also signed what is believed to be the first cease-fire in Chadian history.

An illustration depicting the surrender of Rabih's army after it was defeated by French forces in 1900.

THE FRENCH ARRIVE

In 1883 Kanem-Borno and its neighbors came under the control of a former slave named Rabih Zubar Fadlallah. Throughout the 1880s Rabih conquered and expanded his control over the Kanem-Borno kingdom and its neighbors. He then established his own capital in Dikwa, south of Lake Chad. However, Rabih had made many enemies by defeating many powerful rulers. Some of them had heard about a new power in the area, the French. They allied themselves with the French in hopes of winning back their kingdoms.

In 1898 Rabih's forces fought several battles against an army of French and Baguirmi soldiers. As neither side would concede defeat, the fighting continued for two years. On April 22, 1900, when the two forces met at the Battle of Kousséri, the French forces defeated Rabih's army and killed him. Also killed was one of the French commanders, François Lamy. In his honor, the French named one of their outposts Fort Lamy, which today is Chad's capital, N'Djamena.

The French had a difficult time keeping peace in Chad. The extreme remoteness of the Chadian outposts meant that civil and military authorities had to travel long distances overland to get to their assignments. In 1928 about 45 percent of the civil-service positions were unfilled, as no one wanted to accept an assignment in Chad. To combat this, the French made arrangements with local chiefs, charging them to collect taxes and conscript labor. When this did not work, the French used excessive force to frighten the populace into obedience. Villages were depopulated, animals slaughtered or taken, and crops burned.

The French arrive

In order to make Chad a profitable holding, the French implemented forced labor on farmers to produce cotton. Women were recruited to work beside the men carrying dirt, cutting grass, and transporting stones, as well as cooking and fetching water for the rest of the laborers. Disease, starvation, and exhaustion killed many laborers. Some laborers were driven by hunger to raid nearby villages, thus spreading chaos and lawlessness wherever they were assigned. People deserted their villages to escape the raids. On some occasions, French administrators arrived at villages ready to conscript more labor only to find that everyone was already gone.

Others were taken to serve in the French army. During World War II (1939–1945) the French had an entire battalion composed of Chadians called the Régiment des Tirailleurs Sénégalais du Tchad, or the R.S.T. Casualties were high. Because service in the French army was so dangerous, violent resistance to recruitment was common.

The French also imposed taxes to be paid in cash on a population used to paying their chiefs taxes in kind. A man who raised cows gave a cow, for instance. The tax demands prompted more people to relocate to other areas. Such fugitives were pursued relentlessly. In general, French colonization led to economic disruption and population displacement in Chad.

In the 1920s, 20,000 Sara in the south of Chad, encouraged by their traditional leaders, refused to pay their taxes or provide any forced labor. Their local chiefs promised them that French bullets would turn to water rather than hurt them. Emboldened, the Sara rebelled against the French government. In response, the French killed 5,000 people, razed their villages, and slaughtered all the farm animals. Throughout their tenure in Chad, the French retaliated with excessive force against those who opposed their rule.

The French outlawed native languages, fearing that Chadians would plan revolts in languages the French did not understand. The mandatory use of French left a legacy in Chad: today many people have French names such as Souffrance (Suffering), Tristesse (Sadness), and Douleur (Pain).

A boy rides past a school built by the French.

FRENCH RULE

French rule brought a few positive influences into the lives of the people of Chad. The French built schools and stopped the slave raiding of the south by the inhabitants of the north. The French presence was most strongly felt in the south, while in the Muslim north the Arabs lived in relative autonomy. Though those in the south had to deal with a greater French presence, they also benefited from better access to education, health care, and positions of influence in the government. This led to resentment by northerners, who felt that their needs and concerns were not being adequately addressed. The southerners, meanwhile, kept alive their animosities toward northerners as a result of centuries of slave raiding. After Chad gained independence in 1960, this resentment continued unabated.

Northern and southern Chad were also divided by ethnicity, lifestyle, and religion. In the north, the population was made up of Arabs and groups such as the Tubu. Most practiced Islam and as the region had little permanent water or arable land, most people were nomadic herders. In the south, the Sara were the dominant ethnic group. They were farmers and followed native religions or Christianity. The French called the south *Tchad utile*, or "useful Chad." The north, which is now the BET prefecture, was *Tchad inutile*, "useless Chad" and it contributed little to the economy.

After World War II the French abolished forced labor and made all Chadians French citizens. In 1945 political parties were permitted for the first time. Chadians elected delegates to the French National Assembly, and in 1952 to the Territorial Assembly. Both men and women were allowed to vote, and blacks and whites voted in the same places.

One of the best-known political groups of the time was L'Union Démocratique du Tchad, founded in 1946. It was concerned mainly with Muslim interests and therefore was more popular in the north. To achieve their goals, members of this political party cooperated with parties founded by French people living in Chad.

Parties in the south, such as the Parti Progressiste Tchadien (PPT), were more interested in ending forced cotton production and the French rule. Parties such as the PPT did not seek to cooperate with the French and so were viewed with suspicion by the authorities.

Chadian president François Tombalbaye (*right*), and French president, Georges Pompidou, wave to the crowd in the streets of Fort Lamy (N'Djamena) during the triumph of the PPT in 1959.

The political situation was chaotic during that time. Chadians sought political parties that would, for the first time, represent their own interests rather than the interests of a king or the French. But the result was dozens of parties being formed, each responsible only to a small, core group. A confusing array of parties battled each other for seats in the Territorial Assembly at every election. The PPT, though, began to emerge as a strong party in the north as well as the south.

Despite problems and occasional violence, the first predominantly native government in Chad was formed in 1958. The PPT was in power, but not for long. Within four months, the government had been disbanded and reformed four times under opposition pressure. Finally on June 16, 1959, the PPT under the leadership of François Tombalbaye emerged triumphant and in charge.

25

INDEPENDENCE

Chad gained its independence from France on August 11, 1960. Tombalbaye, who was from the south of the country, led the country from that point until 1975. His regime was noted for promoting southern domination over other regions of the country.

Tombalbaye was the country's first president as well as the leader of its armed forces. He appointed all members of the Supreme Court, all provincial governors (*prefets*), and his cabinet. The country had a National Assembly, but it existed merely to rubber-stamp the president's decisions. Opponents to Tombalbaye's regime were removed from their positions. Some were arrested and sent to prison.

In 1963 during an anti-government protest, 500 Chadians were killed. Tombalbaye declared a state of emergency. Under these conditions, northern Chad grew increasingly restless. Leaders in the south were also unhappy with Tombalbaye, but as he favored them over the north, they grumbled less.

In 1968 Tombalbaye launched his "Cultural Revolution" designed to rid Chad of foreign influences and colonial practices. Street names were changed and the capital, Fort Lamy, was renamed N'Djamena in September 1973. All government officials were required to change their French names to traditional African ones. Tombalbaye himself dropped his first name, François, in favor of Ngarta, which means "chief." On the street, people were encouraged to greet each other as *compatriote* rather than Monsieur.

Some requirements of the "Cultural Revolution" outraged even Tombalbaye's supporters. He ordered the return of a traditional Sara initiation rite, *yondo*, which involved circumcision. During the 20th century, *yondo* rites had largely been abandoned, especially by those who had converted to Christianity. Now government workers who had not been initiated, even those in their 50s, were forced to undergo the rites.

Tombalbaye holds up a flag, marking Chad's independence from foreign influence.

Tombalbaye also arrested dozens of people, including some from his own PPT party, whom he accused of using voodoo magic against him. He weakened the army, brought in foreign advisers for his own security, and hired Moroccan bodyguards. He sometimes boasted he had survived more assassination attempts than any other African leader.

Opponents to these changes, many of whom were southerners, were exiled, arrested, beaten to death, or burned alive. Increasingly, southern voices were raised with northern ones in opposition to Tombalbaye's government. On April 13, 1975, junior officers of the army along with other military personnel launched a coup and killed Tombalbaye.

AFTER TOMBALBAYE

General Félix Malloum became the next president of Chad. He tried to stem the tide of resentment against the government by appointing Muslims to his cabinet and freeing political prisoners. Some rebel groups reconciled with the government, but some, including those led by Tubu leader Hissen Habré, did not. By 1976 Malloum had become the target of assassination attempts.

Violence in Chad continued unabated. During several battles with rebels, nearly 2,000 Chadian soldiers died. To try to stop further rebellion and deaths, Malloum appointed Habré as prime minister in August 1978.

Even though Hissen Habré restored law and order to Chad, he is also wanted by Belgium for war crimes and crimes against humanity.

The two men had vastly different agendas, however, and could not work together. In February 1979 civil war broke out.

By 1986 Habré managed to wrest control over the whole of Chad. Coincidentally, several years of heavy rains brought abundant harvests, and the populace was better fed than it had been in some time. This helped bolster Habré's position. The completion of a bridge across the Logone River, which linked N'Djamena with Kousseri in Cameroon, eased transportation problems. Goods could now be shipped out of the country more easily. Schools were full of children, and the international community began paying more attention to what was happening in Chad.

Habré's tenure as leader of the country was marked by a national army that was better trained and more disciplined than before. It also marked the end of Chad's isolation from much of the outside world, and the return of at least some measure of law and order to the country.

In 1990, however, one of Habré's former supporters, Idriss Deby, gathered a rebel army and captured N'Djamena. Habré fled the country.

Deby tried to re-create a multiparty political system in Chad, and by 1993 there were 26 political parties. In 1996 and again in 2001, Deby was elected president.

Deby's former defense minister, Youssouf Togoimi, began a rebellion against Deby's government in 1998. They signed a cease-fire in January 2002. In 2003 another rebel group in the southeast, the National Resistance Army, agreed to a cease-fire. Despite the official agreements to put down their weapons, not all rebels have done so, especially in the north, which is strewn with many landmines. In April 2006 rebel forces entered N'Djamena in an effort to overthrow President Deby. However, government troops fought back with President Deby declaring, "The situation is under control."

GOVERNMENT

IDRISS DEBY TOOK OVER the administration of Chad in December 1990, promising to promote freedom, justice, and multiparty democracy. Yet it soon became clear that he was in no hurry to fulfill this promise. In 1992 the French withdrew their air-strike force from Chad. Many people believed this was France's way of telling Deby that French support for his administration was contingent on him holding elections in Chad.

In January 1993, Deby opened a conference, called the Sovereign National Conference, that was supposed to draw up a new constitution for Chad. It brought together 176 delegates from numerous areas and backgrounds. Many of them were village or town chiefs, but some were farmers and nomadic herders. Religious leaders and Chadians who had been living abroad were also included in the conference.

The conference appointed an interim government, led by Deby, that was supposed to last for one year. It lasted for three years, but finally, in 1996, Chad had a new constitution and presidential elections were held. Elections were held again in 2001 and 2006.

Left: **Idriss Deby of Chad (*fifth from the left*) attends a ceremony marking Senegalese Infantrymen Day.**

Opposite: **Supporters of President Idriss Deby attend the second celebration of the Senegalese Tirailleurs (Infantrymen) Day, on August 23, 2005.**

فندق ليبيا

KEMPINSK

THE GOVERNMENT

The government of Chad is headed by a president. Since 1990, the president of Chad has been Idriss Deby. The president appoints the prime minister and his cabinet. He also helps to decide on appointments for positions on the Supreme Court, other judicial openings, generals, and provincial officials.

The president must be elected by more than 50 percent of the popular vote and is elected to a five-year term. If no one receives 50 percent of the vote, the two candidates who have the most votes stand in a second round of voting.

The National Assembly, which has 155 members elected by popular vote to four-year terms, is the main body of the legislative branch of the government.

The National Assembly meets twice a year, in March and October. Special sessions may be held as necessary. Every other year the National Assembly elects someone to serve as president of the assembly. The National Assembly may draft laws, which are sent to the president, who has 15 days to approve or reject them.

Appointments to the Supreme Court are for life. The chief justice is chosen by the president. Chad also has a Constitutional Council, which is made up of nine judges elected to nine-year terms. This council reviews legislation, treaties, and all international agreements before they can officially be adopted.

The constitution of Chad allows for the recognition of local traditions and laws, so long as public order is maintained. Equality for all citizens and freedom of religion are also part of the constitutional guarantees.

In the 14 prefectures that make up Chad, many administrative posts are appointed by the president or the minister of the interior. These administrators do not have term limits. Instead they remain in office until they are replaced.

The person in charge of the prefecture, who is called a prefect, is assisted by a group of 10 people who are picked by the prefect and accepted by the minister of the interior. The people appointed to these councils are often tribal leaders or others who have a great deal of status in their communities.

In the 1960s nine towns in Chad were granted municipal status by the government. They generated their own revenue through taxes, fines, and fees. The councils that run these towns are often directly elected by the townspeople. Those who are elected to the council vote among themselves to elect a mayor for the town. Many decisions of these mayors and their councils, however, must be approved by the minister of the interior before they can be implemented.

Chad has more than 5 million registered voters.

A Chadian woman casts her ballot at a polling station outside a Gendarmerie office in N'Djamena.

ELECTIONS

Elections in Chad are different from what they are in the United States. Because most people in Chad cannot read, political parties write songs and have them played on the radio rather than having articles on their policies written up in newspapers. Trucks with loudspeakers will drive through villages and towns, playing the election songs for the various parties. One song for the MPS (the party of Idriss Deby) declares, "MPS, *ma-nikhalu, ballat-na, ma yi-shallu,*" which roughly means, "MPS will not leave or abandon us, nor will they take our vote away." People in the trucks will pass out T-shirts or other gifts to encourage people to vote for their candidate.

On election day, the trunks of trees are painted white as part of the national celebration. As most of the Chadian electorate is illiterate, voters are given pieces of paper, each one with a different candidate's picture on it. At the poll, the voters put their thumbprint on the paper that has the picture of the candidate they wish to vote for. The ink they use to put their thumbprint on stains their finger and proves that they have voted. It also keeps anyone from voting twice.

IDRISS DEBY

Idriss Deby was born in 1952. His father was a poor seminomadic herdsman of the Zaghawa ethnic group. Deby entered the military and was selected for pilot training, which he completed in 1976 in France. He was active in the military after returning to Chad and by 1982 had been promoted to colonel and chief of staff. In 1985 he was sent back to France for a senior officers' staff course.

In 1989 the regime led by Hissen Habré turned on its Zaghawa supporters, killing many. Deby and other Zaghawas in the military fled. Although Deby managed to reach Sudan and then Libya, others were captured and executed. With Libya's help, Deby formed and trained his own army.

In December 1990 he overthrew Habré's regime and became ruler of Chad. Almost immediately, Deby's regime proved to be just as brutal as the one it replaced—human rights advocates and civic leaders were intimidated, political opponents simply disappeared, and many people were arrested for opposing the regime.

Deby's main personal military force, used to intimidate his opponents, is a 2,000-strong group made up almost entirely of his fellow Zaghawas.

Deby did, however, finally fulfill his promise to introduce a multiparty system and presidential elections to Chad. He has now twice been elected president. He ran for president again in 2006 and once again won the election, though the constitution forbids presidents from holding office for three terms.

A CRISIS FACING THE GOVERNMENT

Chad's neighbor Sudan recently emerged from a damaging civil war in 2005. During this time, more than 200,000 refugees fled from Darfur in Sudan to Chad. Internally, more than 1 million people in Sudan have been displaced and have not been able to cross the border.

Most of the refugees arrived without belongings, and settled within five miles of the border. These refugees have had to scrape together whatever food and shelter they can find, and they usually have no sanitation and health care facilities. Because much of eastern Chad is in the Sahara or the Sahel, there are few natural resources. As a result, the Chadians and the Sudanese have been competing for whatever food, water, and firewood they can find. To make matters worse, rebel groups sometimes cross the border to attack the camps. All in all, tensions are high.

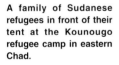

A family of Sudanese refugees in front of their tent at the Kounougo refugee camp in eastern Chad.

The Darfur crisis has also created problems between the army and the government in Chad. Many of the army officers support the rebels in Sudan, as they are from the same ethnic groups, whereas the government has sought to maintain neutrality.

The United Nations' refugee agency, UNHCR, has moved in to build refugee camps, distributing sheets, mosquito nets, and clean water. It also hopes to provide some measure of health care and education to the refugees. Refugees have been moved into 11 camps, and this may help relieve the competition between the Chadians and their Sudanese neighbors.

The crowding and stress of camp life often results in the spread of disease. In some camps in Chad, refugees have been suffering from meningitis. Health workers from the World Health Organization have since vaccinated almost 72,000 people.

A young refugee from the Darfur region of Sudan has his height measured by a health worker in Oure Cassoni, northeastern Chad.

THE GOVERNMENT TODAY

Although many towns and villages have elected mayors, it is often the traditional leader—a chief or a sultan—to whom people turn for the resolution of their property or marital disputes.

Chad still faces problems in turning itself into a democratic nation. The laws of the land are often ignored, especially by the military forces and some branches of the government.

Though the constitution of Chad grants its people civil rights, the majority of its prison population is made up of people who have been arrested and held without trial. People accused of being criminals have been tortured and sometimes executed without trial, and some units of the military are so out of control that they have been accused of killing shopkeepers for their money.

Unlike in the United States, prisoners in Chad are not fed; their families must provide their food. Sometimes the prisoners' visitors can walk up to the jail's windows to hand food over.

Complaints about the treatment of prisoners and other civil rights issues are taken to judges, but many of them have been intimidated by the military or other governmental departments that are committing the crimes. Judges who try to get away from such government interference are dismissed.

There is at least one voice speaking out against the lawlessness that continues to threaten Chad's democracy, and that is the press. The newspapers and journals of Chad are almost uniformly anti-Deby and publish articles critical of him. One journal, *N'Djamena Hebdo*, uses editorial cartoons to ridicule Deby. Although officially Deby claims that Chad has a free press, newspaper offices are sometimes ransacked by government employees, and there have been instances where editors of journals and newspapers critical of Deby have been fined and sued for defamation.

For the moment, *N'Djamena Hebdo* is still being printed. It has won international awards for its advocacy of press freedom in Chad and its struggle to keep the government accountable. It is widely read by those in Chad who are literate, and many of them are willing to voice their opinions about the government, at least with those they trust.

Chad's progress toward democracy since independence has been shaky. Though the government currently supports a multiparty system and presidential elections, some international organizations have voiced concerns over whether the elections in Chad are held fairly. Election laws have been instituted, but some branches of the government regularly ignore them. Although the situation remains unstable, some Chadians, such as journalists, are trying to cast a spotlight on the problems of the current regime.

Idriss Deby prepares to cast his vote for the 2006 presidential elections. He altered the constitution so that he could run in the presidential elections for a third time.

ECONOMY

AT THE TIME of independence in the 1960s, Chad had an economy that was dependent mostly on cotton. Its industry and transportation sectors were small and underdeveloped.

Drought during the late 1960s and 1970s created a huge problem for the country. Farmers were unable to grow enough crops to sell; sometimes not even enough to feed themselves. Without agriculture, the economy was in desperate trouble, and Chad was forced to rely on international aid for its survival.

Several problems continue to keep Chad's economy depressed. It has no harbors, no railroads, and few paved roads. Transporting anything to a national market, let alone an international market, is an expensive, dangerous, and time-consuming undertaking.

Left: **There are few paved roads in Chad, especially in the desert region.**

Opposite: **Water-bearing women passing an oil rig. Profits from oil and other natural resources often do not reach Chad's poor.**

The postal service must rely on trucks carrying goods to market and on people who own cars (such as missionaries) to get mail to outlying towns. During the rainy season, some areas can go several months without mail as the trucks cannot pass through the muddy roads.

Some towns have telegraph operators who know Morse code and are able to get messages in and out of town. Otherwise, during the rainy season, people are largely cut off from help or supplies from outside their village.

LAND MINES

Chad's civil wars and uprisings since independence have left behind many unexploded land mines. Between 1998 and 1999, Chad reported that 127 people had been injured or killed by land mines. However, because most of the people who live in areas with land mines are nomadic, they do not report land mine deaths and injuries to the government. The real number of casualties is therefore probably much higher.

International organizations are trying to find and destroy the mines in order to help the people who live in the areas. They are also concerned for cattle in the region, because if too many of the animals are killed by land mines, the nomads might starve. Also, people are unable to farm in areas with land mines.

Some international groups are training animals to detect land mines. Animals such as the African giant pouch rat take six weeks to train, while honeybees can be trained in two hours. Since neither the rats nor the bees will set off the explosives, using them to detect land mines will save the lives of the people and their animals without risking more lives in the process. Once cleared of mines, the land can once again be used for farming and livestock grazing without fear.

EXPORTS

Cotton is Chad's main export, making up 80 percent of its export revenue. Over 50 percent of the farmers in Chad plant cotton. Chad ranks as the 12th leading exporter of cotton in the world.

Although cotton is native to the region, it was not until the French arrived and required cotton to be grown that it became an important cash crop.

Most of Chad's cotton is exported to Germany. The prefectures of Mayo-Kebbi, Logone Oriental, and Moyen-Chari grow the most cotton and together produce almost half of the country's crop. Cotton is planted around mid-June and harvested in November.

Gum arabic is the resin of the acacia tree used by pharmaceutical and food industries. By 1970 Chad was the fifth largest producer in the world of gum arabic, but drought in the 1970s and 1980s disrupted production.

A cotton harvest in southern Chad.

MINERAL RESOURCES

Chad's industries and economy have not developed sufficiently to exploit the natural resoures found in the country. Natural resources such as bauxite (aluminum ore) in the south and uranium in the north have not been exploited.

In the north, rebels and land mines have kept development away. In the south, industry has not yet developed to mine the bauxite, which is found in Koro near Moundou.

Other minerals have also been found in Chad, such as silver and titanium. Traditionally the only mining industry in the country has been the mining of natron (sodium carbonate) in areas that have dried up around Lake Chad.

Unfortunately, even though cotton farming supports many people, the production of cotton uses so much pesticide that the environment is being damaged.

43

ELECTRICITY

Electricity is needed for cooking, for staying cool or warm, for light, for work, for recreational activities, and for transportation. In Chad, however, fewer than 2 percent of the people have access to electricity. The rest have to burn wood to keep themselves warm, to cook, and to have light after dark.

Chad has only one power station, which is near the capital city. Thus, almost all Chadians who have electricity live in N'Djamena. But because the country must import the fuel needed to run the power station, the station is very expensive to operate. Unfortunately, this means that although Chadians are very poor, they must pay some of the highest prices in the world for electricity.

HIV/AIDS IS AN ECONOMIC PROBLEM

In 1990, 70 percent of the people in the world with HIV/AIDS lived in sub-Saharan Africa, a region in which Chad is located. This area is also where 80 percent of the children afflicted with HIV/AIDS lived. It is estimated that 2.4 million people in sub-Saharan Africa died of AIDS in 2000 alone. That is almost the same as the population of Chicago, Illinois.

The economic impact of this disease has been enormous. HIV/AIDS most often strikes people who are in the prime of their lives. These people are the ones the community depends on to be farmers, herders, office workers, teachers, translators, and soldiers. They are usually the ones who are of child-bearing age. When they die, many children become orphans.

Industries that are needed to move into an area and help spur economic growth cannot find enough workers. People who may be educated enough to work in the civil service are dying just when they are finishing their educations.

Some countries in Africa, such as Botswana, have had to recruit workers from other countries just to fill the jobs that their government and industries need to operate. Skilled workers are often difficult to find because too many people who have received an education and special job training are too sick to work or have died.

In South Africa the absenteeism and loss of productivity caused by sick workers have reduced the country's economic growth rate. By 2010, South Africa's growth will be 17 percent of what it would have been without AIDS. That amounts to a loss of more than $22 billion to the economy just from the impact of one disease. Across Africa, economic growth is expected to drop by 25 percent during the next 20 years due to HIV/AIDS.

The number of homeless children is on the rise due to the AIDS pandemic in Chad.

When people die of AIDS and leave their children behind, many of these children have nowhere to go. Relatives may take them in, but if the children have no living relatives, or if their relatives are too afraid of HIV to take them into their homes, the children become street children. They are forced to beg and steal to survive.

The presence of these homeless children in the villages and cities keeps people from wanting to start businesses or invest in the areas. No one wants to be robbed or beaten by roving gangs of starving children. These children often die very young from drug abuse, alcoholism, violence, or AIDS. So far about 72,000 children have been orphaned by AIDS in Chad.

The medical costs of the disease continue to mount as well. As more people get sick, more doctors, nurses, and other medical personnel are needed to care for them. Most countries in Africa, including Chad, have limited amounts of money to spend on health care.

Already in some countries, the cost of treating HIV/AIDS has risen to 90 percent of the total national health budget. Every other disease and medical condition, from childhood diseases to broken bones to pregnancy, must be funded by the other 10 percent.

This situation can only get worse as more people get infected by the disease, and the 5- to 10-year lag between acquiring HIV and showing the first symptoms of AIDS means that people can go on spreading the disease for years without knowing they are doing so.

Across sub-Saharan Africa, it is estimated that at least 9 percent of the people there have HIV/AIDS. So far Chad has not been as severely affected as some other countries, with 3.6 percent of the people estimated to have the disease. But without adequate means of prevention, Chad could face some of the extreme problems facing other areas of sub-Saharan Africa.

Chad faces many challenges in growing its economy. Uncertainties in the cotton market, the prevalence of land mines, and the increase in the number of people with HIV/AIDS mean that Chad will have to struggle just as its neighbors do to achieve and maintain economic growth.

First Ladies Margueritte Kerekou of Benin and Zena Wezena Derby of Chad (*right*) attend the 2005 African First Ladies summit, which was focused on AIDS and conflict prevention in Africa.

47

ENVIRONMENT

LIKE THOSE EVERYWHERE ELSE on earth, the land, plants, and animals of Chad are vulnerable to overuse and abuse by the humans who live there. Much of Chad is in either the Sahara desert or the Sahel and so has very limited access to water. People in these areas are either farmers or pastoralists who rear sheep and goats. The people, the animals, and the plants all compete for the limited sources of water and food the land has to offer. In the south, although water is more abundant and the rainy season is longer, the problems do not go away. A growing population means there are always more people who need clean water and food.

Many problems plague Chad and other nations that border the Sahara desert, including air and water pollution, soil erosion, and a decline in the variety and number of plants and animals in the region. Unfortunately, Chad is too poor to address many of the environmental problems it faces.

Some organizations, such as the French Office Nationale du Developpement Rural (ONDR) have come to Chad to try to help. The ONDR educates people on how their soil is being depleted through overuse and how they can use different farming techniques to help the soil rather than destroy it. They also teach people how to conserve water, such as by using the water from their bucket showers to water the plants near the house or by planting their gardens in partial shade.

Also, the forestry service in Chad taxes and restricts the use and shipment of wild products such as honey and wood. By doing this, the government hopes to cut down on the amount of resources people extract from the fragile Chadian environment.

Above: **Sandstorms are common in this remote Chadian part of the Sahara desert.**

Opposite: **A caravan passes by the Rocks of Archai in the Sahara desert.**

Villagers draw water from a well in the Sahara desert. Water is scarce in many such regions.

SUB-SAHARAN AFRICA

The forty-seven countries located south of the Sahara desert, including Chad, constitute sub-Saharan Africa. Sub-Saharan Africa has one of the highest population growth rates in the world, at approximately 2.2 percent per year. In contrast, the United States had an estimated growth rate in 2005 of 0.92 percent. By 2025 it is projected that sub-Saharan Africa will be populated by nearly a billion people if the estimates are correct.

The international community is concerned about the environmental problems in this region. In 2002 South Africa hosted the World Summit on Sustainable Development, which was held to address issues such as water, sanitation, energy, and health. It was the first conference that included energy problems in its discussions. Because of this conference, the United States pledged to contribute $4.5 billion over three years to help improve the health conditions and enable access to clean water for people in sub-Saharan Africa.

One reason for the conference was that small groups of citizens in sub-Saharan Africa had begun to organize and highlight issues to their governments about their local conditions. When people learn how and why their local environment is being damaged, they are often eager to help fix it but may not have the resources to do so.

One problem is that past projects that have been implemented to help people, such as the drilling of wells, have not been followed up on. After the government or an international organization has provided the resource and left it behind, it will inevitably deteriorate to the point where no one can use it anymore. Today more groups are recognizing the importance of teaching the locals how to maintain and repair the equipment so that the funds invested in local development do not go to waste.

THE CHAD-CAMEROON PIPELINE

One of the greatest threats to Chad's environment is the Chad-Cameroon pipeline. Chad's biggest economic development has been the discovery of oil. Income from oil sales will make up half of Chad's income every year. Chad must export its oil to other countries if it wishes to help its citizens climb out of poverty, yet this very thing also threatens its environment.

The pipeline project was started by oil companies in 2000, led by ExxonMobil. They formed a coalition to build a 663 mile (1,067 km) pipeline that would carry oil from Chad to Cameroon. The Chad-Cameroon pipeline was completed in 2003 and cost approximately $4.1 billion. To help the people of Chad, the oil companies and the government of Chad brought in the World Bank as an investor and guarantor. This means the World Bank could impose conditions on the oil companies and the Chadian government. It also provided more than $200 million for the construction of the pipeline.

A soldier stands guard at a Chadian oil rig.

To calm investor's fears that it would take the money without building the pipeline, the Chadian government requested that no money be transferred to the country until all the banking arrangements and conditions placed on the revenue had been approved and finalized. Until the money is

51

disbursed, it is held in a bank account outside the country. According to the agreement, 10 percent of the oil revenue will be held in the account for future generations.

The agreement that governs the pipeline and the revenue it will generate covers only the three oil fields of Miandoum, Kome, and Bolobo. In September 2004 the Chadian government issued a statement that future oil development will continue under arrangements that have the same conditions.

From the revenue the oil will generate, $19.3 billion has been earmarked to be spent on road improvements. Two major roads, Bisney-Goura and Ngoura-Bokoro, will be paved. Also, $4.9 billion has been allocated to education. Most of the money will go to build classrooms and buy books, desks, and other supplies for students.

People whose houses were in the way of the pipeline were offered $1,000 or compensation in-kind in the form of equipment, bicycles, sewing machines, and fruit trees. Because of the remoteness of some regions, cash is not always as helpful to people as such supplies. The total amount paid out to individuals was roughly $12 million for the affected areas in both Chad and Cameroon. Besides payment to individuals, payments were also made to communities to offset the economic losses they faced due to the construction of the pipeline.

Some villages were promised schools; others were promised wells, because nearly 75 percent of the population does not have access to safe drinking water. The World Bank offered to lend the money to Chad in exchange for promises that 80 percent of the money gained from oil revenues would be spent on infrastructure, public health, social welfare programs, and education; 5 percent on local development near the pipeline; and 10 percent to be held for future generations. The rest will be used for general expenditures.

An oil refinery in Kome. The boom in the oil sector represents a new lease on life for Chad's economy as it is estimated that an additional 80 million dollars of revenue will be generated annually.

Chad received its first oil revenues in 2004 in the amount of $84.6 million. This increased Chad's national income by 31 percent in 2004 alone. Chad expects continued double-digit growth in its income, entirely from revenue from its oil exports.

In October 2005 Chad's government announced its plans to break its agreement with the World Bank by passing new legislation concerning the oil revenues. If passed, the fund for future generations would be scrapped and the oil revenue will not only be channeled to areas such as agriculture, education, and health care, but also to military spending.

The government also planned to change the law to allow it to spend up to 30 percent of the oil revenue. These actions have angered officials at the World Bank as well as members of civil and human rights organizations in Chad. Some are also worried that the new laws and increase in military spending reflect instability from within Idriss Deby's government.

Humans are not the only ones liable to suffer from the creation of the pipeline and the reallocation of oil revenues. Though the pipeline brings money to Chad, it also threatens wildlife such as chimpanzees, gorillas, and elephants. These animals live in the rain forest that the pipeline passes through. Chimpanzees and gorillas are endangered species. Scientists estimate that they will exist in the wild only for 10 to 50 more years if nothing changes. Some people estimate that the African elephant will be extinct in the wild within 10 years. In the end, while the pipeline may bring revenue to Chad, the consequences of its construction and continued presence may leave the country with more liabilities than benefits.

Endangered species such as gorillas can be found in rain forests, which are situated along the Chad-Cameroon pipeline.

EXTINCTION

Animals and plants become extinct for several reasons. They may be killed by people for food or destroyed because they are in the way of human development. Another reason could be that a new species is introduced to the region, and it breeds faster or uses resources better than the species that were there before. This new species may have been brought by people, or the seeds of plants may have blown to a distant area by the wind.

A third way animals become extinct is through the side effects of human activity. When we cut down forests for timber and firewood, or drain swamps to build houses, we destroy the homes of many animals. Some of them cannot survive anywhere else and will die off.

Animals such as the elephant and the chimpanzee are threatened because people are destroying the areas where they live and because the production and shipping of oil through the pipeline result in soil contamination.

PEST CONTROL

Locust control is very important in the Sahel region, which includes large parts of Chad. Locusts are a kind of grasshopper that eats any plant they come across. Swarms of the insects often sweep across Africa, devouring everything they find, which leaves farmers, who are making a meager existence from the land, with nothing. Just one locust swarm can affect millions of people in many countries.

Seven African countries, including Chad, are cooperating with the World Bank's International Development Association for the Africa Emergency Locust Project, in order to find ways to control the damage caused by locusts in the future.

Each country will be responsible for its own strategy to limit and contain locust swarms and save crops. In 2005 all seven countries involved in the project had specific locust-control plans in place.

The Africa Emergency Locust Project is keeping tabs on the plans of all seven countries to guarantee that there are no overlaps or gaps in the locust-control coverage area.

In April 2005 locust-control specialists from each of the seven countries met in Mali, to review their plans together with the World Bank, the Food and Agriculture Organization, and other agencies. So far the World Bank has approved spending $12.4 million to support African locust-control efforts.

One way to control locusts is by spraying pesticides on the swarms. The pesticides kill the locusts but also pollute the plants and the ground. Still, because it is an effective means of control, nearly 42,500 square miles (110,074 square km) of land in Africa was sprayed in 2004.

Scientists continue to search for ways to control the unpredictable outbreaks of locusts so that subsistence farmers in Chad will not need to fear a loss of their livelihood every summer.

In the future, people might be able to control locusts by other means. For instance, people might use a fungus, *Metarhizium anisopliae*, which is deadly to locusts. It is thought to be harmless to other insects, plants, animals, and people.

Scientists seek to control the locust swarms and do not want to eliminate them entirely. Locust swarms are part of the natural cycle of the region, and no one is sure what the side effects would be if they were eliminated entirely.

There are other pests, such as birds called millet eaters (*mange-mille*), which plague some areas of Chad. During the past few years *mange-mille* populations have skyrocketed. This is caused in part by the Chadians' fear of snakes. Chadians kill snakes when they see them, but many of these snakes eat the birds' eggs.

Locusts cover the ground.

The birds multiply rapidly when their main predator is gone. More eggs survive to hatch, and more baby birds survive to adulthood. They then eat the millet that the farmers depend on for their survival.

Chadians are beginning to realize the importance of their natural environment. Many ecological problems have arisen as a result of economic development. As most Chadians still rely on the land for their livelihoods, problems such as these will not only threaten natural wildlife but also entire communities as well. Steps taken now can guarantee the future of the soil and the water, and thus secure the future of the people of Chad.

Bush fires add to the threat of extinction for Chad's natural wildlife.

CHADIANS

MORE THAN 200 DISTINCT ethnic groups can be found in Chad. This diversity is often cited as one reason nation-building has been slow to take root in the country. Many people feel their first allegiance is to their own group, not to the nation at large.

THE SARA

The largest ethnic group in Chad is the Sara. The Sara are sedentary farmers and fishermen living in the south of the country who are divided into clans. A few of the clans are the Gambaye, the Mbai, the Goulaye, the Madjingaye, and the Kaba, though there are many others.

The main social group among the Sara is the lineage, or family—called the *qir ka* among the eastern Sara, the *qin ka* among those living in the center of the region, and the *qel ka* among the western groups. Lineage names refer to the male ancestor of the people in that group. People identify with the lineage of their father, and rights to land are passed on from father to son.

The main social unit of the Sara is the extended family, which includes all married and unmarried brothers, their unmarried sisters, and their children. Family members may live in an enclosure together, with many such family units forming a village. Each family within the enclosure manages their affairs independently from other families in the village.

If all the people of a Sara village are from the same lineage, the village may be led by a single group of elders. If several lineages share a village, elders from the different groups will often come together to try to resolve problems between lineages. In such cases, the elders from the lineage that first moved into the area have senior status.

Very few Sara have converted to Islam. Catholic and Protestant missionaries have converted many, but some Sara still follow their native

Opposite: **A Chadian girl leads her younger sister back home. Older Chadian children usually help their parents look after the younger ones.**

A Chadian family living in the Tibesti region. Homes are usually round in shape and made of straw.

religion. Because of their proximity to the French-controlled districts of Chad, some Sara saw the opportunity for education that could lead to positions in the armed forces and civil administration. Even today many positions of authority within the government are still held by the Sara.

Noi is the name of a small Sara caste whose members function as priests. The Noi do not marry outside their caste, and their numbers are estimated to be fewer than 1,000. The installation of a Sara village chief requires the services of a Noi.

THE TUBU

The Tubu live in the north of Chad. The two main branches of this ethnic group are the Teda and the Daza. Historically they have been antagonistic toward each other and do not recognize each other as part of the same tribe.

The Tubu herd animals and cultivate crops at oases. Some mine for salt. Tubu families are formed by the parents and their children, and perhaps other relatives who need a place to stay. They travel with other families in bands, but membership of the bands change from season to season.

Every Tubu belongs to a clan. Identifying with a clan is important as it establishes a person's place in Tubu society. Within a clan, everyone counts his or her descent from the same ancestors and shares the same cultural symbols and taboos.

Clans have recognized ownership over certain natural resources such as palm groves, springs, and pastures. Other clans may not use these resources without permission.

Conflicts between families only affect family honor, not the honor of the entire clan. If a Tubu is murdered, the victim's family will often seek revenge on either the killer or his or her relatives. Failing that, negotiations will secure the payment of a *goroga*, or blood price, which is often paid in camels. When men take more than one wife, the wives are usually from different clans and will have their own separate living quarters.

A Tubu chief (*seated*) of the Tibesti Tubu tribe Kinimi Ede-Mi.

THE HADDAD

The Haddad clan lives in the north of Chad. They speak the local language of wherever they are found and do not have their own common language. The Haddad keep to themselves, live on the fringes of others' villages, and rarely intermarry with other ethnic groups.

They are skilled workers who are often involved in iron working, weaving, dyeing cloth, tanning leather, and making shoes. Their neighbors often despise and fear them, however, because of the menial work they do and because they are said to practice magic.

A Haddad metalworker begins his work under the shade of a tree.

THE FULANI

The Fulani are nomadic and seminomadic herders who have converted to Islam. They refer to themselves as Fulbe and call their language Fulfulde. They first settled in what is now Chad in the 15th century. After their conversion to Islam, their settlement at Chekna became a center for religious studies for Fulani from all over Central and West Africa.

The Fulani raise cattle and farm millet and corn. A family needs about 100 cattle to be self-sufficient. The corn, which ripens more quickly than the millet, provides food while the Fulani wait for the millet to ripen. Millet and milk are the most important foods in the Fulani diet.

The Fulani do not live in settled villages but often roam with their cattle during the rainy season. During the dry season, cattle are concentrated around the few remaining water holes and are kept on the fields where, during the rainy season, the Fulani grow their millet. Thus the cattle manure fertilizes the fields during the dry seasons.

If the rainy season is a bad one, however, there might not be enough rain to saturate the soil, and the large quantities of cattle manure on the fields often lead to fires, making the land unusable for several seasons. Men tend the cattle, while the women are usually less nomadic, building houses in small clusters near water holes.

A woman will collect the materials to build her house herself, but her friends, family, and children may also help. The house is considered to belong to the woman, as are the responsibilities for household duties such as raising the children and cooking.

The overriding bond in Fulani society is between mother and child, not between man and woman as it is in the West. A Fulani man looking for a wife will seek someone who will be a good mother to his children. For the first few years of life, a young child will be always within arm's reach of its mother.

A child either will be with its mother while she works at home or will be carried on her back if she needs to go out. A baby who cries is immediately picked up and nursed. A Fulani woman who lets her baby cry is considered a bad mother.

Fulani herders draw water from a well for their cattle.

Fulani children wearing colorful headscarves.

Though the Fulani are Muslims, they do not speak Arabic, and few send their sons to Koranic schools. Those who are educated in Koranic schools are well respected, but people often would rather ask a village elder for advice.

Many Fulani carry charms and believe in magic. Most know how to prepare love potions. Men are said to use them to get women to love them, while women use them to keep their husband's eyes from wandering. Most women do not want their husband to take more wives, even though this is customary.

The Fulani see marriage as a gradual process rather than something attained in a single ceremony. During the betrothal, the bride will be taken to her future husband's mother's house where, on several occasions, she will run back to her father's house. This process goes on for some time until the two are living together on a regular basis. But the marriage is still not considered complete until the first son is born.

Like other Muslims, the Fulani pray five times a day. But they do not necessarily pray at the same times of the day as other Muslim groups.

The government of Chad has had a difficult time getting people from different ethnic groups to come together as a unified nation. The multitude of ethnic groups and languages has been a barrier to creating a peaceful Chad. As Chad emerges more prominently on the international stage, however, the people of the country will have good reason to work together harmoniously for a brighter future.

LIFE EXPECTANCY

The life expectancy of Chadians is one of the lowest in the world, yet it is on the rise. In 1964 life expectancy was 29 years for men and 35 years for women. By the late 1990s it had risen to 43.9 years for men and 47.1 years for women.

Compared to the United States, this figure is still very low and reflects the lack of adequate health care and proper nutrition among Chadians. Although the government is trying to address these issues, Chad continues to face major problems in trying to ensure that all Chadians have access to health care, clean water, and adequate food supplies.

LIFESTYLE

LIFE IN RURAL CHAD is very different from life in the urban area of the country. Very few people have access to electricity, and most people do not own cars. The majority of the population live in small villages in mud or straw huts and cook on a wood fire. The people grow crops or herd animals so that they can feed their families.

In a Chadian village, men are more noticeable than women. They take on leadership roles and most teachers, doctors, and nurses are male. Communities are run by the men, and they are often the sole breadwinners of their families.

In the cities, people own luxury items such as bicycles, cars, radios, and televisions. They dine at restaurants and go to the movies. Urban dwellers usually work for the government, banks, or for private businesses. Walking down the street of a Chadian city, are people going to work, restaurateurs inviting people inside their establishments, and store-owners offering their wares for sale.

Above: **Two Chadians put their finishing touches on a thatch hut.**

Opposite: **Chadians shop in a busy market in N'Djamena, the capital of Chad.**

WOMEN IN CHAD

In Chad women have very different lives from most women in the United States. They are expected to have large families, and girls have very little access to education or modern conveniences.

Women often get up very early to perform household chores such as sweeping their courtyard. Later in the morning they go to the market to exchange surplus goods or produce for the items they need for their home. Afternoons are often filled with work such as grinding grain or shelling peanuts. Women will often sing and joke with one another as they perform these routine tasks to make it more enjoyable.

A girl sells milk at the market. Most Chadian girls do not have access to an education and have to work to support their families.

Women are often the ones who work the land. They plant and tend the sesame, peanut, and millet crops. If there are loads to carry, women will carry them on their heads, even if they are very heavy. They must also gather wood, make fires, and cook for their families.

Many Chadian women are widows, their husbands having died due to war or disease. That leaves them to do the household work and also somehow earn enough money to make up for whatever wages their husbands would have brought home. Sometimes women have other family members who can help them, but their lives are still very hard.

Women usually have many children. Unless a woman is very lucky, at least one of her children will die due to some childhood disease or accident. The older children will often have to help around the house and also take care of their younger siblings allowing their mother to get more work done.

CHILDREN IN CHAD

Children living in the capital city are more likely than others to go to school. Even so, they can also be found helping their families by selling vegetables and fruits in the markets. They may also help their mothers look after younger siblings, cook the meals, and clean the house.

Children must walk to and from school, as there is no public transportation to get them there. The school is likely to be in a one- or two-room building with walls made of clay and a roof of tin. The teachers will have students from multiple grades at the same time. While the teacher is working with one age group, the others will be busy with their own assignments.

The teacher rarely gives the children homework, as most children will be busy at home helping their parents. There is always so much to do around the house that the children are needed to help out whenever they can. During the rainy season, when the seeds must be sown, the children will not go to school, so that they can help their parents in the fields. Having many children is expensive but it also means the parents have more hands to help in the fields, or with herding the animals, or in the family business. Fathers will teach their sons how to help in their offices or shops.

Children have time for play, but they learn about their responsibilities to their families at a young age. Whether it is gathering firewood, drawing water from a well, sweeping the house, or baby-sitting a younger brother or sister, every child has a role to play in a Chadian family.

There are school breaks during the planting and harvesting seasons so that the children can help their family in the fields. Even young children are sent out into the fields for days at a time to line strings along each row of the crop. The strings are decorated with strips of bags, wire, or

Most children in Chad have six or seven brothers and sisters.

69

other shiny things. The child sits in the shade and waits for the birds to come and try to feed on the crops. When the birds come, the child pulls the string, and the birds fly away, startled by the flapping things on the string.

FAMILY

Chadians are very concerned with family. Adult children often live near their parents, and elderly people usually live with or near one of their sons. Polygamy is very common, even in Christian areas. Children of the same mother and father are usually very close, and they are also likely to be close to their half-sisters and half-brothers. All children by the same father are considered brothers and sisters, even if they have different mothers. People use the term "cousin" when referring to members of their extended family.

Chadian children are expected to take care of their younger siblings.

Extended-family members are important when people wish to find jobs or a place to live in a new town. People will often call upon their distant relatives when such help is needed.

In the family, men make the important decisions while women are in charge of the house and domestic responsibilities. They cook, sew, and raise the children. Women in the south have more freedom to travel and are more likely to have their own money compared to women in the north, where Muslim families often keep their daughters and wives inside family compounds, which they cannot leave without permission. Southern women may earn money by selling milk, yogurt, and spices in the market.

A Muslim family in eastern Chad.

Young people rarely date, as many marriages are arranged by their families. Girls are expected to help their mothers as soon as they are able and they are unlikely to have much free time as they have to take care of their younger siblings, too. By the time they are teenagers, girls are expected to marry.

Men may wait until their 20s to find a wife because many ethnic groups in Chad require the young man to give a gift, or dowry, to the bride's parents before he can marry their daughter. It may take the young man some time to accumulate this dowry, so he will most likely be somewhat older than his bride. During the time the young man is raising the dowry, he will get to know the woman's father and brothers; once he has done that, he will be able to spend some time with his intended bride.

Local celebrations, such as weddings, can be time-consuming but festive affairs; however, some weddings can consist of a simple payment of a bride price to be considered complete. Among some groups in Chad, a couple is only considered married once the woman becomes pregnant.

WEDDINGS

In the south, women in the village usually take a week to make preparations for a Christian wedding. They sit on straw mats in small groups and chat while they sift flour, grind wheat and millet, and fry dough into something similar to doughnuts. Goats and chickens are killed and their meat prepared. Meanwhile, children are running around squealing and getting underfoot, and the women sing songs and clap their hands. The atmosphere is very joyous.

During this week of preparation, one night is set aside for people to form a line and present gifts to the bride and the groom. The gift might be a goat or a sheep. Other common presents are household items such as pots, pans, other cooking utensils, bowls, and soap. After the gift-giving, the men perform traditional dances wearing animal furs and sing celebratory songs.

On the day of the wedding, the bride and the groom ride in a car while the entire village walks behind. Everyone goes to the church for the ceremony. Some people will stick their heads in the windows so they can see what is going on. A few elements of the wedding ceremony have been borrowed from the West: the bride often wears a white dress, and the couple kiss at the end of the ceremony.

Muslim ceremonies last for days and include a great deal of feasting and gift-giving. Islamic law allows a man to have up to four wives at once, but he must treat them all equally. New wives are often seen as rivals by the first wife and will not be welcomed, though sometimes co-wives manage to get along well.

A young Chadian couple pose for their wedding photographs.

Two Fulanis participate in a horse race held during a wedding in Bousso.

Muslim weddings are considered to be a contract between two people made in the presence of Muslim witnesses and the bride's father or guardian. The groom is required to give the bride a dowry. The dowry can be cash or something else, such as herd animals if that is what the groom possesses. The gift will be specified in the marriage agreement, though the actual payment can be put off until a later date.

The bride may or may not be present when the contract is made. If she is not present, her father or guardian must ask her in the presence of two witnesses if he has her permission to make the contract with the groom and if she agrees to the dowry that has been proposed.

EDUCATION

Formal, structured educational programs were not introduced to Chad until 1920, two decades after it came under French control. Such programs began small, and progressed slowly. By 1933 Chad had only 18 trained teachers. The largest school had only three grades and 135 enrolled students.

By the 1950s enrollment had climbed to more than 17,000, the bulk of whom were in public schools. In Christian areas private schools had been established by missionaries, but no such private schools were available in the Muslim areas of the country. This was due to Muslim resistance to sending their children to Western-style schools and because boys were already being educated in Arabic at small Koranic schools, which provided religious instruction and some general education. For many people, this was sufficient education. Also, lessons in public schools were taught in French, which was not spoken by many people. Students entered school only to be confronted by a language they did not speak at home.

More children have the opportunity of going to school now but the number of boys still outnumbers girls in class.

Most of the students sent to school by their parents were boys. Parents usually did not consider an education for girls necessary, since girls could only look forward to a life of marriage, childcare, and taking care of the family's home. But boys were not much better off. At best, schools offered only a few years of instruction. Literacy rates remained very low.

By the time Chad became independent in 1960, there were only three secondary schools in the entire country. Student enrollment in Chad was only about 11 percent. Anyone who wanted to get an education had to have the means to leave the country. Since most people make their living through subsistence farming, they could not afford to get more than the bare minimum of an education for their children.

Chad took a big step in the early 1970s with the founding of the University of N'Djamena. Due to the outbreak of hostilities in the late 1970s, however, the university was closed in 1978. The campus was looted during the 1979 and 1980 battles in the capital. Teachers went back to their home villages and returned to farming while the civil wars raged.

The university reopened in 1984 and had 1,500 students by 1988. But because schools had not been staffed by trained professionals and the students' education had been interrupted by years of violence and uncertainty, students were unprepared for academic studies. In 1994, 86 percent of secondary students failed their university entrance exams.

Today the situation has improved and the university has three faculties: the Faculty of Arts and Human Sciences, the Faculty of Law and Economics, and the Faculty of Pure and Applied Sciences. Degree programs include history-geography, modern literature, French, English, and Arabic, mathematics and physics, and biology-chemistry-geology.

Primary education in Chad consists of a six-year program. Once completed, the student earns an elementary-school certificate. In the

Fortunate Chadian students who seek university educations go to France, Belgium, Senegal, or the Ivory Coast.

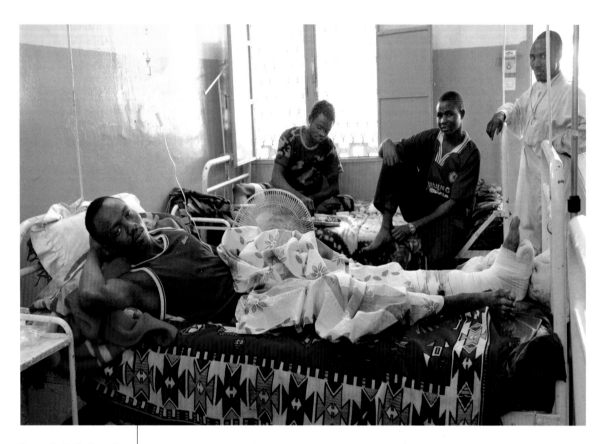

Due to the limited number of hospital beds, only a small percentage of Chadians have access to health care.

south students often start school at age 6; in the north they are often older. Subjects include reading, writing, spelling, grammar, mathematics, history, geography, science, and art.

Secondary education in Chad follows the French model. Students who have their elementary certificate compete to get into two types of schools the college or the lycée. The college offers a four-year course, the lycée a seven-year course. At the end of these terms, the students take exams that are a requirement for entry to the university.

HEALTH CARE

Most people in Chad do not have access to modern health care. One of the diseases facing Chadians is meningitis, which can be caused by bacteria or viruses. The viral forms are not usually life-threatening. However, the bacterial forms, including meningococcal meningitis, are extremely dangerous. The bacteria enter the body through the nose and the throat and travel to the brain, where they cause swelling of the membranes that surround the brain and the spinal cord. Symptoms include headache, fever, a stiff neck, and sometimes vomiting and confusion. The disease can result in permanent brain damage, hearing loss, learning disability, limb amputation, kidney failure, or death. Bacterial meningitis can be treated with a number of effective antibiotics. In 2005 the international medical humanitarian aid organization, Doctors Without Borders, launched a meningitis vaccination campaign in eastern Chad, following a recent outbreak among refugees from Sudan's Darfur region. The campaign aimed at protecting the people

Chad is within an area spanning sub-Saharan Africa known as the "meningitis belt," where epidemics affecting thousands of people occur regularly. In Chad alone, outbreaks have occurred in 1998, 2000, and 2001.

A doctor examines a sick Sudanese refugee child as his mother watches in eastern Chad.

Due to the cramped conditions in refugee camps, diseases such as meningitis are easily communicable.

from the highly infectious disease, which is particularly threatening in the overcrowded refugee camps.

Meningitis is often spread during the hajj season as pilgrims make their way to and from Mecca. During the 1988 hajj season, meningitis spread from Ethiopia to Saudi Arabia, to Sudan, and finally to Chad. More than 4,500 cases were recorded in N'Djamena alone.

Additionally, childhood diseases such as whooping cough, measles, and polio that are routinely prevented in more-developed areas of the world, are a major problem in Chad. With enough vaccinations, these diseases could be controlled, if not eliminated entirely. Unfortunately, in some areas of Africa, including Chad, many people have boycotted the polio vaccine.

Amid rising Muslim-Western tensions, Nigeria's Muslims led the immunization boycott. This boycott triggered an outbreak all across the continent, infecting children in neighboring countries including Benin, Chad and Cameroon.

A heath care worker vaccinates children against polio in northeastern Chad. International aid agencies set up hospitals and vaccination centers to contain the spread of polio in Africa.

Polio is a disease that affects the nervous system and is carried via contaminated water. It causes paralysis, atrophied muscles, and sometimes death. Although anyone can contract polio, young children are the ones most often affected.

Each year in Chad, more than 60,000 children die from disease or hunger before they reach the age of five. Getting health care to the people is difficult without the necessary infrastructure. There are no educational institutions to train healthcare workers. Chad's remoteness also means that health care must be delivered by truck or small airplane, and many people simply do not have access to those few places where health care is dispensed. Approximately 30 percent of Chad's population had access to health care in 1990. Today, that number is only slightly higher.

In the 1980s the entire country could boast only five hospitals and 18 medical centers. A total of 3,500 patient beds were available for a far-flung, diverse population of millions. The addition of a few private facilities later raised that figure to 4,200 beds.

RELIGION

MANY PEOPLE IN CHAD continue to follow native traditions in one form or another. Practitioners of these native religions view the world as a complicated system of relationships among people (both living and dead), animals, plants, the forces of nature, and supernatural powers. All things are considered to have some sort of life force. The relationships among all these life forces are well-ordered and hierarchical, so that each has its own recognized and established place in the universe.

According to these religions human societies reflect this hierarchy. For instance, people live with families, families live in villages, and villages are headed by chiefs or a council of elders. Everyone has a place and lives by rules and laws that allow everyone to get along. People who break the rules or commit crimes act against this natural order. Their deeds invite bad luck because the order, once upset, will remain upset until it is rebalanced. If people act in an antisocial manner by disobeying the rules of their society, they invite chaos to attack the village—perhaps the crops will fail or the animals will sicken and die. Ritual acts such as prayers, sacrifices, and dances can restore the balance to the natural order. Restoring order protects the people as well as their families, animals, and crops.

Ancestors are a very important part of this balance. They are seen as being able to intervene directly in human affairs because they bridge the gap between the natural world, having once been alive, and the supernatural world, being dead. The ancestors most prone to intervene are those who have recently died, since it is believed that it may take weeks or months for the newly departed spirit to fully cross over into the land of the dead. Many rituals are designed to appease these new spirits.

People follow certain practices to help them avoid the attention of bad spirits. They do not allow a child to sleep alone inside a house because

Native African traditions are animistic. Animism is the belief that all people, animals, plants, and objects have souls or spirits.

Opposite: **A young Chadian boy wears a charm around his neck to ward off evil.**

an evil spirit may steal the child away. Nor will they compliment a child on his or her looks for fear of making a bad spirit jealous. Also, people will not whistle after dark, because it could attract the attention of wicked spirits.

The Sara celebrate the harvest by going through the newly harvested fields with nets and fire, trying to catch the ancestors. The ancestors are then offered plenty to drink, while the living eat the first meal made with the new crop.

OLD RELIGIONS AND NEW

Many Chadians practice both a native religion and an imported religion such as Islam or Christianity. The native religions sometimes feature a creator god who made the universe and then retired from intervening in its affairs. This is why people appeal to spirits, who play active roles in this world, rather than to this god.

Yet because the belief in a creator god is already part of native traditions, people often find Christianity or Islam easy to embrace. They do not see a problem with believing in the Christian god and yet turning to the ancestors and the spirits for guidance or assistance. For instance, a Muslim

DIVINE RULERS

Human rulers were often considered to have divine powers given to them by the spirits. The Moundang believe that their leader, the *gon lere*, has the responsibility of maintaining a good relationship between humans and the spirits who live in the sky. Similarly, the *mbang* (chief) of a Sara village is likewise in charge of intercessions with the spirits in order to maintain and renew the social order.

may pray to Allah (God) but wear a charm or drink ink that was used to write verses of the Koran to ward off disease or evil spirits.

Whatever their religion, most Chadians believe in magic and witchcraft. Some people act as magicians to help others determine the will of the spirits. Most people would not hesitate to consult such people. Magicians are able to use magic, which can be bad or good, to help or harm. Everyone knows who the magicians are; they can be asked to help someone get his or her health back or to bring good luck. Sorcerers, however, work in secret because their magic is always evil and they use it to siphon away and consume the energy of others.

When people suspect a sorcerer is nearby because bad luck or disease has struck a village, they will consult a magician to identify the sorcerer and find a way to stop the disruption of the natural order. A sorcerer, once revealed, will be punished, and rituals will be performed to appease the spirits and return the universe to balance.

ISLAM

Islam was founded by the Prophet Muhammad in the seventh century. Islam requires its followers to submit to Allah, which can be shown by

following the five pillars of the faith. The five pillars are the performing of daily prayers, the giving of alms, fasting during Ramadan, participating in the hajj to Mecca, and believing that there is no god but Allah and that Muhammad is his prophet. The word of God as revealed to Muhammad is found in the Muslim holy book, the Koran. The sayings of Muhammad are collected in the *hadith*.

People in Chad observe the five pillars of the faith a little differently than other Muslims do. For example, public prayers may take place more often than the usual once a week, and it rarely, if ever, takes place inside a mosque.

During the centuries since its founding, different sects have arisen within Islam. One of them is Sufism, which is differentiated from other forms of Islam by its insistence on achieving direct personal experience with the divine. Some Muslims believe that Sufis are not really Muslims at all, but Sufis believe that they are practicing a pure form of the religion by adhering to its original traditions. A Sufi seeks the truth, which he or she believes can be found only within oneself. Sufis are divided up into brotherhoods, or orders, that attempt to spread Islam throughout the world. Some of these brotherhoods can be found in Chad.

One Sufi order in Chad is the Sanusiya. The brotherhood originated in northern Libya in the 19th century. Their members advocate a return to the fundamental principles of Islam and avoidance of foreign influences. Unlike other orders, the Sanusiya reject music, dancing, singing, and all forms of luxury.

In the mid-20th century, another order, the Tidjaniya, became predominant in Chad. This order was favored by the French throughout their tenure due to the religion's focus on submission to earthly authorities. It was fully established in Chad by the 1950s. However, a new wave of

Islamic fundamentalism from Sudan has weakened the influence of the Tidjaniya in Chad today.

One reason Islam may have had better luck in attracting African converts than Christianity was that native religions often allowed a man more than one wife. Also, Islam was associated with the successful traders who came across the Sahara, while Christianity was associated with the hated colonial government.

The traders looked like the Chadians, dressed like them, spoke their languages, and also shared a similar culture. Thus, Chadians were more receptive to the Islamic religion. Christian missionaries did not have the same advantage.

Although recently an influx in fundamentalist Islamic teachings has found some followers in Chad, so far their numbers are small. The calls for French to be removed as a national language and for all governmental proceedings to be held in Arabic have gone mostly unheeded.

CHRISTIANITY

Christianity arrived in Chad in the early 20th century. Protestants arrived around the early 1920s and the first Catholic missionaries arrived in 1929. But organized efforts to convert the Chadians to Catholicism did not begin until 1946.

The Protestantism first brought to Chad was a fundamentalist version of Christianity from the United States. These missionaries frowned upon dancing, alcohol, and local superstitions. Early converts found it difficult to remain in their native villages because they were not able to take part in many aspects of village life, such as harvest rituals and communal prayers. Thus, the early Protestants often had few converts, as the strictness of their religion did not win people over. Few were willing to give up their families and home villages for this foreign religion.

As more missionaries arrived, however, they set up schools and hospitals. They taught French, which enabled people to find work in the civil service of the colonial administration. These factors encouraged people to convert, and by the 1940s and 1950s, more people were attracted to Christianity. By 1980 Chad had approximately 80,000 Christian converts. These were mainly from the south, as the missionaries did not go to the heavily Muslim occupied areas of the north.

The late arrival of Catholic missions to Chad came as a result of politics. In the early 18th century, the Vatican had declared that Catholicism would be brought to Chad by Italian missionaries, but it was the French, not the Italians, who were in control of Chad. It was only after World War II ended in 1945, that the French Roman Catholic missionaries came to Chad.

Like Protestants, Catholics encouraged education and provided social services. In the 1980s it was estimated that some 20,000 Chadians attended Roman Catholic schools. Many nuns who were sent to Chad were trained nurses who served in hospitals and clinics. This helped some people accept and convert to Catholicism.

Today, most people who are Christian in Chad practice a blend of their native traditions with the imported traditions of the Christian faith.

Above: **A cathedral in the Chari-Baguirmi Province in Chad.**

Opposite: **A Catholic priest conducts Sunday Communion at Abeche.**

RELIGIOUS TENSIONS

Most of the time, the various religions of Chad exist side by side with few problems, but sometimes tensions boil over. For instance, in February 2003 a Christian church in Abéché was burned. In 2002 the Catholic Church was formally admonished by the minister of territorial administration for attempting to combine religion with politics, which is illegal under Chad's constitution.

It is not always Christianity that receives rebukes from government officials, however. In 1998 and again in 2001 the government banned the Sufi group Faid al-Djaria, which it accused of following un-Islamic

A priest greets his parishioners after a Sunday service.

customs such as allowing men and women to interact with one another during religious ceremonies.

While a few people who have converted to Christianity from Islam have been shunned or even beaten by their families, the government itself does not force anyone to convert to any religion, nor have any incidents been reported in which terrorist organizations targeted religious establishments in the country. Religions like Baha'i and Jehovah's Witnesses have been allowed into Chad, though they have not yet found many converts. Religious teachings are forbidden in public schools, but religious organizations are welcome to open schools of their own.

A Chadian man prays along the road to Abeche. Muslims have to pray five times a day.

LANGUAGE

THE OFFICIAL LANGUAGES of Chad are French and Arabic. Many people in Chad are not conversant in either Arabic or French, but they may speak three or four of the native languages found in their immediate area.

More than 120 languages and dialects are spoken in Chad. Many of these languages have never been extensively studied or are little known to the outside world. Some are spoken only by a few people of one ethnic group. Others, like the Sara language in the south, are spoken by large numbers of people. But when people from different areas of the country meet, they often have to use French or Arabic to communicate.

The presence of such a diversity of languages suggests that Chad was a crossroad for many migrations in the past. As people passed through the area, some moved on and some stayed, contributing to the diversity of different languages.

ARABIC

Arabic is spoken by more than 220 million people in the world today and is the official language for more than 20 countries. It is written from right to left and has 28 letters. Some of these letters have four forms—the forms they take at the beginning, the middle, or the end of a word, and the form they take when appearing alone. This can be confusing for people used to the Roman alphabet.

Arabic is a Semitic language. Few Semitic languages are still in use. Of those few, Arabic is by far the most widespread and widely spoken.

Above: **A grocery store in Kouba displays a signboard written in French.**

Opposite: **The official languages of Chad, French and Arabic, are taught to children in schools.**

A child writes Arabic script on a small chalk-board.

The others, such as Hebrew, which is spoken in Israel, and Amharic, which is the official language of Ethiopia, are some of the few Semitic languages that are still in use. Arabic is so widespread because it is the liturgical language of Islam. All Muslims are supposed to be able to read the Koran in the original language, which is classical Arabic. Many of these people, when they converted to Islam, learned Arabic for their everyday use as well.

Children sent to Koranic schools are taught classical Arabic and its script. Because the spoken Arabic of their area can be very different from the classical Arabic they learn in school, students are not necessarily able to read and write either modern standard Arabic or their local Arabic dialect upon graduation. They will know only classical Arabic.

More than 30 dialects of Arabic are used in Chad. They are spoken mostly in the north of the country. Arabic was introduced with Islam in the 14th century; The Arabs of Chad divide themselves into three groups: the Juhayna, the Hassuna, and the Awlad Sulayman. The Juhayna arrived in the 14th century. The Hassuna came after them, and the Awlad Sulayman did not migrate to Chad until the 19th century. The Hassuna and the Awlad Sulayman, most of whom were herders or farmers, migrated from the area that is today Libya.

Because many Arabs earned their living as merchants, Chadic Arabic (also called Turku) became a trade language across the country. Until the 1970s much of the business in non-Arab towns, such as Sarh and Moundou, was conducted in Arabic. After the sectarian violence in the late 1970s, this practice was discontinued in some areas.

Arabic is also spoken among groups who are not Arab by ethnicity. Some of them were probably former slaves of Arab masters, such as the Yalna and the Bandala, but others have adopted the language after long exposure to Arabic-speaking neighbors.

Did you know many English words, including "algebra," "cotton," and "magazine," come from Arabic?

SOME COMMON WORDS IN ARABIC:

Yes	*Na'am*	No	*La*
Thank you	*Shukran*	Good morning	*Sabah al-Kheir*

Some words and phrases in Arabic change depending on whether one is speaking to a man or a woman. For instance:

Please	*Min fadlak* (to a man)	*Min fadlik* (to a woman)
Pardon me	*Samehni* (to a man)	*Samehini* (to a woman)
How are you?	*Kif halak?* (to a man)	*Kif halek?* (to a woman)

THE ARABIC ALPHABET

The Arabic alphabet today has very ancient roots. It was developed from an Aramaic script used more than 2,000 years ago. But Arabic has more sounds in it than Aramaic, so people could not use the alphabet as it was. Over the centuries, speakers of Arabic languages adapted the original alphabet into something that was more useful to them. The current form of the alphabet was developed around the seventh century A.D.

Arabic is usually written without vowels or marks to indicate pronunciation (diacritical marks). However, the Koran is written with both because it is considered the word of Allah, and Muslims believe proper pronunciation of the word of Allah is vital.

The letters of the Arabic alphabet look very different from those being used in this book. They are:

English	Arabic	English	Arabic	English	Arabic	English	Arabic
'(a)	ألف	d	دال	ḍ	ضاد	k	كاف
b	باء	ḏ	ذال	ṭ	طاء	l	لام
t	تاء	r	راء	ẓ	ظاء	m	ميم
ṯ	ثاء	z	زاي	ʿ	عين	n	نون
ğ	جيم	s	سين	ġ	غين	h	هاء
ḥ	حاء	š	شين	f	فاء	w	واو
ḫ	خاء	ṣ	صاد	q	قاف	y	ياء

The numbers used in Arabic are also different. Unlike words, which are written from right to left, numbers are written from left to right.

zero	٠		six	٦
one	١		seven	٧
two	٢		eight	٨
three	٣		nine	٩
four	٤		ten	١٠
five	٥			

CHARACTERISTICS OF ARABIC

One characteristic of Arabic is that it has what are called "sun letters" (*shams*) and "moon letters" (*qamar*). The Arabic word for "the" is often written in English as *al*. When a noun begins with a moon letter, the definitive article remains *al*, as in "*al-qamar*," the moon. When a noun begins with a sun letter, the word *al* changes its *l* for the initial consonant in the noun thus, the sun is known as "*ash-shams*."

Another feature of Arabic is its three-consonant roots. Any word that has the same three consonants in the same order will be about the same thing. Thus, any word with "k-t-b" will be about writing: *kitab* means "book," *kitub* means "writers," *maktub* means "letter," and *maktabbeh* means "library."

A young Muslim man transcribes the Arabic script of the Koran.

FRENCH

More than 75 million people in the world speak French as their primary language. Another 128 million people speak it as a secondary language. This makes French the 11th most spoken language on the planet.

"Francophone" describes countries where French is spoken as the first or second language by the majority of the population. Chad, therefore, is part of what is called Francophone Africa, since French is one of its main languages.

French was introduced into the area in the late 19th century. When the French gained control of the area, it became the official language of government and of institution. At that time, Chad was part of what was called French Equatorial Africa.

COMMON FRENCH WORDS AND PHRASES

Do you speak English?	*Parlez-vous anglais?*
Excuse me	*Excusez-moi*
Glad to meet you	*Enchanté*
Good-bye	*Au revoir*
Good evening	*Bonsoir*
Good day	*Bonjour*
How are you?	*Comment allez-vous?*
I don't understand	*Je ne comprends pas*
I'm sorry	*Désolé*
Please	*S'il vous plaît*
Thank you	*Merci*
You're welcome	*De rien*

French remains a very important second language for many people in Chad. Government documents and Web sites are generally in French. About 1,000 French expatriates live in Chad.

SARA

Many people in Chad speak some dialect of the Sara language. Sara dialects are spoken in the region between the towns of Moundou and Sarh. Sara is a tonal language and has three tones: ascending, flat, and descending. Tonal languages are very hard to learn because the same sounds spoken with different tones will mean different things.

A billboard in French urges Chadians to vote for Idriss Deby.

In Sara, *mang* said with a flat tone means "ox," but pronounced with a descending tone, it means "buy," and when said in an ascending tone, it means "cigarette." Someone whose first language is English, French, or Arabic may not be able to discern the differences and this can be confusing for them.

Sara has words for only three colors—black, white, and red. Every other color is described by using the word *nyere* (color) and then an object of that color. A yellow bowl could be called "a bowl the color of the sun," or a green shirt might be "a shirt the color of a leaf."

Aside from the usual languages like Arabic, French, and Sara, English is slowly being introduced into Chad with the arrival of international aid agencies.

Some people use French words for colors that have no name in Sara. Also, there is no word for "thank you" in Sara, so many people have adopted the French *merci*.

Sara also has the interesting feature of having a double plural form that is, some plural words can be made plural again. For example, *de* means "a person," and *dege* means "people," but *degege* means "a group of people."

Chad is a land that has a wealth of languages. This means that most people must learn at least a portion of a second language such as French, Arabic, or Sara just to talk to people from other towns or areas. This diversity in languages makes Chad a fascinating place.

COMMON SARA WORDS AND PHRASES

Hello	*Lapia*
Goodbye	*Aou lapia* (literally, "Go well")
Goodbye	*Indi lapia* (meaning "stay well," the response to *aou lapia*)
How are you?	*I baing?*
I'm fine	*Mto kari*
House	*Kei*
Food	*Yan kessa*
Eat	*Issa*
Drink	*Aing*
Fire	*Por*
Friend	*Maade*
Play	*Ndam*
Give me water to drink	*Adoum man maing*

ARTS

CHAD HAS ALWAYS had strong traditions of music and practical arts such as pottery and leather-working. Through these arts, people compose songs that bring people together and make items that people can use in their everyday life that are both practical and beautiful. But Chadians are also adapting old traditions, like storytelling, in new ways, such as telling stories on film. Chad is just beginning to be recognized internationally for all it has to offer the arts.

TRADITIONAL ART

More than 80 percent of Chad's population is employed in subsistence farming or herding. Most of these people have little contact with the area outside of their immediate homeland. Their handicrafts, although constantly improving and changing, belong to local traditions that have been in existence for hundreds of years. These arts include woven mats, wood carvings, leather products, jewelry, and wool rugs.

Chadians also make baskets, mats, and fans from straw. One widely practiced craft is that of carving calabashes (a type of gourd). The calabashes are etched with many intricate geometric shapes and used for household purposes or turned into musical instruments.

Potters make items such as clay pots and cups by using coils of clay added one at a time on top of each other. Gradually the pot takes shape under the potter's skillful fingers. After the pots are finished, they must be put into a fire so that they will harden. The potter keeps watch on

Above: **Brightly colored hand-woven cloth for sale at a market stall in N'Djamena.**

Opposite: **A man weaves a mat from palm leaf strips at Lake Chad.**

Early examples of Chadian art can be found on rocks and walls of caves in Archei.

the fire, and when it is very, very hot, he covers the fire with sand. By morning the potter will have his wares ready to take to market.

Also, women are adept at embroidery and men at carving leather statues. People also weave tapestries and carve objects from soapstone. They make these items to sell to earn a little money. People take their items to a market, where they are often traded to merchants to sell to others. These merchants often are Arabs, who have been the dominant force in trade in Chad for centuries.

Traditional musical instruments include trumpets made from the horns of goats, a kind of harp called *kinde,* and a tin horn called a *kakaki.* An instrument that uses calabashes is the *hu hu.* Among the Sara, people use whistles, large drums called *kodjos,* and *balaphones,* which are something like xylophones.

The traditional music of the Sara combine flutelike sounds with drums. The music of the Baguirmi people more often combine drums with zithers. Zithers are sound-boxes that have 30 to 40 strings and are played with fingers, a bow, or a plucking instrument. The Baguirmi also have a traditional dance which involves the use of grain-pounding pestles, which they pretend to use on the other dancers.

LITERATURE

Though few Chadians have attained a high level of literacy, several writers of note have come from Chad. Joseph Brahim Seid is a Chadian writer and politician. He wrote books now considered classics in Chad, including *Au Tchad sous les étoiles* (*In Chad under the stars*, 1962) and *Un enfant du Tchad* (*A Child of Chad*, 1967), based on his own life. Baba Moustapha left a posthumous publication, *Le Commandant Chaka* (1983), in which he denounced military dictatorships.

A close-up view of a balaphone, a popular traditional musical instrument of the Sara.

Koulsy Lamko is another writer from Chad. He was born in 1959. His works include a collection of poems, *Aurore* (2001); a play, *Corps et Voix: Paroles Rhizome* (2001); and a novel, *La Phaléne des Collines* (2000). A poet, Nocky Djedanoum, who was also born in 1959, has published a collection of poems on the Rwanda genocide in *Nyamirambo*, which was presented at the Fest'Africa in 2000. Djedanoum was the director of the Fest'Africa that year.

FOLKTALES

Like people around the world, Chadians enjoy telling stories and passing them down from generation to generation. They mix traditional tales with things found in the modern world.

Chadians enjoy gathering together for a chat and it is during such times that folktales are passed down orally from one generation to the next.

One story tells how dogs came to live with people. Long ago, the dog lived with the jackal in the wilderness. But it was so cold one night that they thought they might die, so they looked around for a solution. The dog noticed a village and decided to steal a burning branch from a fire the villagers had started. But instead of stealing the branch, the dog stayed in the village because the people shared their food with him. So the dog got to eat and warm himself by the fire.

Meanwhile, the jackal kept calling for the dog to come back with the burning stick. But the dog told the jackal that he would only come back to the wild when his nose was dry, that is, after he was dead.

Other stories tell people how to live. One story is about a monkey who rescued a hyena from a well. After the monkey took the hyena home, the hyena wanted to eat him. The monkey evaded the hyena and managed to trick him back down into the well, where the hyena drowned. Such stories with morals—which in this case is, "don't hurt the people who help you" teach people how they are expected to behave in society.

PROVERBS

In addition to stories, people around the world also like to repeat favorite sayings. You may be familar with the saying, "The grass is always greener on the other side of the fence," which means that people tend to think that what others have is better than what they have. People in Chad also have favorite sayings.

A few Teda sayings:
Kûdi hi gûshi labannuín.
"Don't let the dog guard the ribs." Do not put untrustworthy people in charge of something you want to keep safe.

Wûroei nôushi gunu.
"Precaution is not fear." Preparing for danger is not the same thing as being afraid of it.

Aba murdom yidado, ba murdom yidannó yugó.
"Anyone with 10 fingers has at least 10 relatives." Everyone has people they can count on.

A few Sara sayings:
Ngon àw mba tá, gèr mba. "A child first goes on a trip, then discovers a stranger." If people stay at home, they never learn about others. To learn about other people, you need to travel outside your hometown to meet them.

Áá kä döi tä à, kä ji tä òso.
"If you notice what is on your head, you'll drop what is in your hand." You cannot pay strict attention to more than one thing at a time.

Bbètä kä bbi äsà mänjo àlé.
"The monkey who sleeps does not eat beans." If you're lazy, you will not have anything to eat. Much like "The early bird gets the worm."

Gòwró kä ngon ì kä kùmänèé.
"Even a small squash has seeds." In a meeting, even a child should be able to have a say.

CINEMA

At least two Chadians have become film directors of international renown. They are Issa Serge Coelo and Mahamat-Saleh Haroun. Both now live in Paris.

Issa Serge Coelo was born in N'Djamena in 1967. He studied in Paris but what he really wanted to do was direct films about his home country. His first feature-length film was *Daresalam* (2000). The movie follows two childhood friends, Koni and Djimi, who flee their village after the government soldiers destroy it because the villagers are too poor to pay their taxes. Koni and Djimi join a rebel band, thinking they will be able

A screen shot from Issa Serge Coelo's *Daresalam.*

to transform Chad into a better place and help those who are denied justice. But as they spend more time with the rebels, they realize the rebels themselves are more interested in power than in helping people.

The film director shows this by having both the government officials and the rebel leaders speak to the main characters in French, a language of occupation, rather than in their native tongue. Ultimately Koni and Djimi come to different conclusions as to how Chad can really be helped and how high the cost is. In the end, the young men find themselves foes on opposite sides, physically disabled and morally at a loss.

In 2001 *Daresalam* was shown at film festivals in Berlin, San Francisco, Moscow, London, and the African Film Festival in New York. Before this movie, Coelo worked on a short film, *Un Taxi pour Aouzou*, which won several awards at film festivals in 1997.

Mahamat-Saleh Haroun was born in Abéché in 1961. He fled Chad during the civil wars, settling first in Cameroon and then in France. At first he worked as a journalist, but his interest soon turned toward telling stories through film. He made two documentaries in the early 1990s and finished his first feature film, *Bye, Bye Africa,* in 1999. The film won several prizes at international film festivals. His second film, *Abouna (Our Father,* 2002), was filmed in Chad and tells the story of two young boys who go looking for their missing father. Haroun cast native Chadians, none of them actors, in his film. He even allowed the child playing the elder brother to choose the boy who would play his younger brother, as he believed that the bond between the children would work better on film if it was already present in real life.

Haroun is adamant about making more movies in his home country even though there are hardly any professional actors there, no film technicians, and no resources to fund film production. The director believes that the people of Chad, who usually watch foreign films dubbed in French, if they see movies at all, will not identify with the Europeans or Americans they see on the screen. He wants them to see images of themselves and to experience on film, stories that are about their lives and what is important to them.

Watching a movie is a communal experience in Chad. A movie night happens when someone who owns or borrows a television and a generator acquires a movie to show. The people in the household then advertise that they will be showing the movie and will be charging an admission price of a few cents. Adults and children will come to the home, carrying

Mahamat-Saleh Haroun (*seventh from the left*) at the 58th Cannes Film Festival.

their own chairs or a mat, and watch the movie outdoors on the television when it gets dark. Many of the films seen by Chadians in this way are Japanese kung-fu movies, and everyone would have seen the few that are available so many times that they can memorize all the dialogue, even though it is in Japanese!

CHAD AND INTERNATIONAL ART

Chad is beginning to emerge from the chaos of its civil wars and onto the international stage for the arts. In 2003 the Arts et Medias d'Afrique held its 10-year anniversary celebration in Chad. The arts festival featured more than 100 writers and artists who showcased their work around the theme "Peace And War: What About Commitment?" The aim was to review African literature of the 20th century, to discuss the state of artistic production and the place of writers and artists during times of peace, and to strengthen artistic ties between Africa and the West Indies.

Other topics, such as HIV/AIDS and its impact on Africa, were also discussed. The festival also featured a carnival to mobilize local talent in N'Djamena, an outdoor cinema, and concerts involving musicians from Chad.

LEISURE

MOST CHADIANS are very poor and have little resources for organized sports and activities such as going to the movies, watching television, and reading comic books. Many of them live without electricity and so they have no computers, telephones, or electronic games. But that does not mean no one in Chad ever has any fun!

Most households have battery-operated radios, and a few may even have a cassette or CD player. Most adults have bicycles to ride, although most children do not.

SPORTS

Chadians are very fond of sports. One of their favorites is soccer, which is called football in Chad. The country sponsors a national soccer team that competes internationally.

Left: **Most women in Chad have little leisure time and have to work hard for a living.**

Opposite: **Two young men play draughts, a board game, using broken pieces of tiles as game pieces.**

A soccer game on a grass field.

In 2003 Chad's national soccer team ranked 156th out of 194 participating countries.

Chad's best athletes are young men who may have often faced hunger, childhood diseases, and other hardships that athletes from most other nations have never had to face. As a result, they may not be as large and strong as soccer players from other nations. However, that does not mean they do not love the game as much as other soccer players do.

Teams from wealthier countries can get companies to sponsor them, and can afford to hire the best trainers and coaches. Chad's team does not have many of such resources.

During the 2002 season Chad was defeated 1–4 by Algeria's team. Chad's lone goal was scored by a substitute player, Naama Naay. After 10 years on the circuit, the Chadian team has yet to win a match when it comes time to qualify for the Nations Cup. However, nearly everyone in Chad follows the team's accomplishments on the radio. Even if their team

TOYS

Most Chadian children make their own toys and amuse themselves with whatever they can find. They will create things from wire, clay, or tin cans. When boys play soccer, they are usually barefoot and will use a ball made of rags bound together or formed from plastic bags. Girls will play with dolls, jump ropes, and jacks (using stones instead of metal jacks), as well as games that involve clapping. Both boys and girls enjoy hide-and-seek.

does not win, people are eager to listen to the games and want to know how their players are doing.

In the cities, boys play basketball as well as soccer. They also play handball and participate in track and field activities. Schools organize their own teams, as do some companies. Local teams will play against one another throughout the year. High schools choose their best players to enter the annual Semaine Culturelle Sportive, which is a national sporting competition.

IN THE VILLAGE

On Sundays and market days in the south, people gather for dancing and enjoy *bili-bili*, a beer derived from millet. People in N'Djamena will also visit the cinema, restaurants, or open-air bars to relax and talk with their friends. Men will play cards or checkers, while women braid each other's hair or embroider. In the villages, people enjoy storytelling, drumming, and dancing in the evening, while in the cities they will visit dance clubs and bars. Still, because acquiring enough food to eat is a problem for many, most people in Chad do not have a lot of leisure time, especially in the small towns and villages.

Elderly people will still be needed to work in the fields and care for the animals. And older children sacrifice whatever play time they may have in order to sell peanuts, mangoes, eggs, or soap in the market to make a little money.

Chad may be a poor country and the people hardworking, but they still find the time to relax with their friends and family after a hard day's work. Just like other people around the world, family and friends are very important to Chadians. They enjoy having the chance to sing or dance together. Women like to embroider, knit, or crochet. This sort of activity is enjoyable but also produces goods the women can sell at the market to help their family.

Childhood is usually short in Chad, with children being given more and more responsibility as they get older. Children often have to make their own toys and invent their own games. Adults and children alike nonetheless find the time to chat, braid hair, or play soccer. Life in Chad is often difficult, but people have fun whenever they can.

Left: **A boy shows off his clay mobile phone. Most children do not have the luxury of store-bought toys and have to make do with what is available. to them.**

Opposite: **Chadian children enjoy a game of cards.**

FESTIVALS

CHAD has eight official holidays: New Year's (January 1), National Day (April 23), Labor Day (May 1), Africa Day (May 25), Independence Day (August 11), All Saints' Day (November 1), Republic Day (November 28), and Christmas (December 25). Many people in Chad also celebrate Muslim holidays such as Eid al-Fitr, Eid al-Adha, and Eid al-Maulud (Birthday of the Prophet).

Opposite: **Fulbe males participate in the Gerewol Festival, which celebrates male beauty.**

HIJRI, THE ISLAMIC CALENDAR

The Islamic calendar is based on the phases of the moon. Each month begins with the sighting of the first crescent moon which usually appears a day or so after the new moon. The year is 12 months long, but because it is based on the moon rather than the sun, it is not the same length as the Gregorian year, which runs from January 1 to December 31. The Hijri is 11 days shorter than the Gregorian calendar.

The actual beginning of each month is difficult to predict in advance, since the months do not change until the crescent moon is sighted by Muslim authorities. Therefore each month can have either 29 or 30 days.

The 12 months of the calendar are:

Muharram	Rajab
Safar	Sha'ban
Rabi al-Awwal	Ramadan
Rabi al-Thani	Shawwal
Jumada al-Awwal	Dhu al-Qi'dah
Jumada al-Thani	Dhu al-Hijjah

The seven days of the week are:

As-sabt (Saturday)	Al-arba'a (Wednesday)
Al-ahad (Sunday)	Al-Khamis (Thursday)
Al-ithnayn (Monday)	Al-jum'a (Friday)
Al-thalatha (Tuesday)	

A Muslim pilgrim prays at Arafat, a pilgrimage site just outside the holy city of Mecca.

MUSLIM RELIGIOUS FESTIVALS

HAJJ One of the most important things a Muslim is supposed to do is to complete a pilgrimage to Mecca, in Saudi Arabia, but only if he or she has the financial means to do so. This pilgrimage is called the hajj. The annual hajj season occurs near the end of the year, during the month of Dhu al-Hijjah. Every year, up to 4 million people travel to Mecca to participate in this observance. The pilgrims include Muslims from many countries, including Chad.

Before the trip, the pilgrim is required to dress in special clothes called *ihram*. These clothes are made of two sheets of white unhemmed cloth and include sandals. By wearing the same clothing, the pilgrims, regardless of their wealth or social standing, show their equality with one another.

Once the pilgrim arrives in Mecca, he or she must circle the Kaaba seven times in a counterclockwise direction. The Kaaba is a shrine that is the most sacred location in Islam. After circling the Kaaba, the pilgrim walks between the hills of Safa and Marwa seven times. This completes the "lesser hajj," or *umrah*. The pilgrim can now go home or continue with the "greater hajj," or Al Hajjul Akbar.

To complete the greater hajj, the pilgrim must do three more things. He or she must go to the hill of Arafat and spend an afternoon there. The time spent at Arafat is usually devoted to prayer and contemplation. After this, the pilgrim goes to the city of Mina, where he or she collects stones to throw at three pillars that represent the devil. After stoning the devil, the pilgrim walks around the Kaaba seven more times. A pilgrim who has completed the hajj may attach the title *al-Hajj* or *Hajji* (Pilgrim) to his name (for female pilgrims, it is *Hajjah*).

The most important festival of the Islamic calendar happens at the end of the hajj season. It is Eid al-Adha.

EID AL-ADHA In Chad, Eid al-Adhal, or the Festival of Sacrifice, is sometimes known as Tabaski. It takes place on the 10th day of Dhu al-Hijjah at the end of the hajj season. Celebrating Tabaski shows a Muslim's commitment, obedience, and devotion to Allah. In the Koran, Allah asked Abraham to sacrifice his son, and when Abraham took his son Ishmael to the place of sacrifice, Allah provided a sheep to be sacrificed instead. In memory of this, many Muslims will sacrifice a sheep on Tabaski. Families who do not have sheep may sacrifice a goat or some other animal. The family who owned the sacrificed animal keeps only one-third of the meat and distributes the rest to other family members, friends, and the poor. Because of this custom, many people who are too poor to afford meat are able to eat it at this time of the year.

Tabaski lasts several days. During this time people socialize with their friends and family, and everyone enjoys special meals of favorite dishes and wonderful desserts. Sometimes children are presented with gifts and sweets to mark the festival.

RAMADAN AND EID AL-FITR Another way in which Muslims show their devotion to Allah is to fast from sunrise to sundown during Ramadan, the ninth month of the Islamic calendar.

At the end of Ramadan, Muslims enjoy the three-day festival called Eid al-Fitr, which celebrates the good things Allah has given them. During

In Christian and Jewish traditions it is Isaac, not Ishmael, whom Abraham is asked to sacrifice.

Ramadan, Muslims may pay a voluntary tax in food or money that is given to the poor so that they can celebrate Eid al-Fitr with everyone else.

Many people who have the resources put up decorations in their homes during Eid al-Fitr and everyone who can afford it will have new clothes to wear. People go to special early-morning prayers in large open areas or mosques. Although Muslims are supposed to pray every morning, special prayers are offered during Eid al-Fitr.

Celebrations begin after everyone gets home from prayer. Children may be given small amounts of money, which ideally is brand new, just like their new clothes. People begin visiting one another around mid-morning, and at each stop they eat special cakes. Since people want to visit many extended family and friends, the visits are very short. The occasion is very joyous, and everyone visits as many people as they can.

Dinner is spent with family, and then everyone goes visiting again in the evenings. The streets are full of music, dancing, fireworks, and games

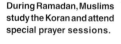

During Ramadan, Muslims study the Koran and attend special prayer sessions.

to celebrate this important festival. By the end of the holiday, both the children and the adults are exhausted from all the preparations, eating, and visiting. Eid al-Fitr is one of the highlights of the Muslim year. Even if a family cannot afford to give gifts of money or to decorate their home, the celebratory spirit of spending their time together and cooking with their friends and family members makes Eid al-Fitr a festive time.

CHRISTIAN HOLIDAYS

CHRISTMAS Christmas is celebrated a bit differently in Chad than in the United States. People do not put up Christmas trees, and Santa Claus is not a popular part of the holiday. Many people are too poor to buy toys for their children, and most of them probably do not live near a store that sells toys in any case. But Chadians still enjoy the Christmas season very much.

Unlike many parts of the world where Christmas presents take center-stage, attending church services or Mass is the highlight of Christmas in Chad.

What is important about Christmas in Chad is the spiritual part of the holiday. People celebrate by visiting one another, sharing special meals, and being thankful for their family and friends. Artists may paint nativity scenes, and since many people do not have electricity, they will not have Christmas lights, but they may put up garland or other homemade decorations.

Choirs perform Christmas songs at gatherings and people sing Christmas carols as they do in the United States. Instead of turkey or ham, people will eat goat or sheep. They attend church services on Christmas Eve and everyone looks forward to spending an entire day with their family the next day.

121

EASTER The Easter season is the most important time in the Christian calendar, since it is the season leading up to the death and resurrection of Jesus. Churches will conduct special services, including services on Ash Wednesday, Maundy Thursday, and Good Friday. But the real celebration comes on Easter Sunday, when Christians go to church to celebrate Jesus' resurrection from the dead. At church they sing songs of joy, sometimes accompanied by drums or other instruments.

At Easter some Catholic churches perform mass baptisms. All the people who are to be baptized dress in white and after Mass everyone goes from the church to the home of each newly baptized person. If 20 people have been baptized, then the whole church ends up at 20 different houses. At each home, people eat and sing hymns. They also sing while walking from home to home.

After church services, people gather with their families to eat Easter meals. If they have a job in the city, they will have the Monday after Easter off to stay home with their family as well.

GOVERNMENT HOLIDAYS

Africa Day on May 25, commemorates the founding of the Organization of African Unity in Addis Ababa, Ethiopia. Many African nations observe Africa Day as a holiday. In Chad some people celebrate Africa Day with contests, sports, and dances. On Independence Day, August 11, Chadians mark the anniversary of their independence with speeches and flag-raising ceremonies.

On holidays people decorate the streets by painting tree trunks white and hanging flags and banners everywhere. Holidays recognized by the government are often celebrated with parades that feature people performing native dances. Important people in the government will make speeches. The parades, speeches, and decorations are indicators of the celebratory spirit.

Another date celebrated in Chad is the International Women's Day on March 8. Although almost unknown in the United States, this is one of the main holidays in Chad. On this day, women form their own parades, race bicycles, and participate in soccer matches. In a festive spirit of celebration, men dress as women and serve food to the women, who are dressed as men.

Every year a new fabric is designed to honor International Women's Day, and women across the country buy this fabric to design their holiday outfit. Thus women from all corners of the country will be wearing the same fabric on this day. International Women's Day is also the one day of the year when most women will go to bars and restaurants.

A common practice of some young people in the capital is called *pari-vente*. A young woman, or a group of young women, will rent a bar for the day and sell alcohol, hoping to make a profit. They will invite all their friends and family to participate, but others are also welcomed. Although the government does not approve of this custom, it is still practiced in the non-Muslim parts of N'Djamena.

Festivals in Chad are celebrated for both religious and secular reasons and are wonderful opportunities for friends and family to get together and eat wonderful meals. As do other people around the world, Chadians consider their families to be very important and appreciate the time they can spend with their loved ones during these special celebrations every year.

To mark International Women's Day, these women dress in their most colorful ethnic costumes.

FOOD

THE NATIONAL DISH of Chad is *boule*, and many Chadians eat it almost every day. *Boule* is a kind of porridge most commonly made of millet (in the south) or corn (in the north), shaped into a ball, and dipped into sauce. Cassava, rice, or sorghum can also be used to make *boule*. Chadians eat a variety of sauces with their *boule*, though the basic ingredients of okra, garlic, red pepper, dried tomato flour, and bouillon are included in most of them. In the north sauces tend to be spicier and have more meat in them. One of these northern sauces is called *nashif*, and is made with spicy tomato sauce and chopped beef.

A similar dish to *boule* is *bouillie*, which is made from millet and peanuts, and is flavored with lemon and sometimes sugar. The result is a milky porridge that is drunk either cold or warm. It is usually served as a breakfast dish but may be served at dinner as well. It is one of the special foods fed to pregnant women, children, and people who are sick, much like chicken soup is in the United States.

Left: **Women sell fruits, vegetables, nuts, and legumes at the market.**

Opposite: **A rural Fulani woman making butter from milk.**

MILLET

Millet is a grain that is not usually eaten by people in the United States. Most people in the United States are probably more familiar with millet as an ingredient in birdseed. The small, white and red spherical seeds in the birdseed mixtures are millet seeds.

In some parts of the world, millet is an important grain that people eat nearly every day. Millet matures rapidly, so it will grow even in very short growing seasons. It is tolerant of dry climate and poor soil conditions. It can also be stored for a long time, so people can keep stocks of millet in case of famine.

Millet was first cultivated in northern China around 4500 B.C. The Chinese considered it one of their five sacred crops. Millet was also cultivated in Africa, probably in the area that is now Ethiopia, and in ancient Egypt. Today people grow more than 6,000 varieties of millet across the world. Many of these are grown to be fed only to animals. The ones most often consumed by people are pearl millet, finger millet, golden millet, fox-tail millet, Japanese millet, Teff millet, and ditch millet.

COMMON FOODS AND BEVERAGES

Peanuts (called groundnuts in Chad) are one of the most important elements of the Chadian diet, along with sorghum and millet. Most of the peanuts grown are consumed locally, with only 3 to 5 percent sold to mills. People use raw peanuts and peanut butter in many of their recipes.

Many people in Chad eat fish, but due to the lack of refrigeration and transportation, it is usually dried or smoked before being sold at the markets. *Banda* is a popular smoked fish cut into segments and exported to Nigeria, Cameroon, and the Central African Republic. The Hausa, Kotoko, and Bornuan ethnic groups commonly prepare it. Nile perch, called *capitaine* in Chad, is a fish that weighs more than 100 pounds (45 kg). It is often exported to Europe, though many people in Chad also like to eat it. At the beginning of the rainy season, people go fishing for *balbout*, a kind of catfish.

The most common meat Chadians eat is goat. Beef is served on some occasions, but most cattle are used for milk production and are not slaughtered. When beef is eaten, most Chadians can only afford to give each person in the family only two or three bites.

Milk is sometimes heated and mixed with sugar, or turned into yogurt or butter. Fruits such as guavas, bananas, and mangoes are available seasonally, especially in the south. In the north people like to eat dates. Rice and pasta are less commonly served compared to millet, and a family will reserve them for special occasions.

Peanuts are a common ingredient in Chadian dishes.

Though we think of the peanut as a nut, it is really a legume and thus closely related to the pea.

Many women will make their own beer, which is called *bili-bili*. Its basic ingredient is millet. Beer is popular with many southern Chadians. The town of Moundou is the home of the Gala Brewery, which produces more than a million barrels of beer annually. The brewery remained in operation even during Chad's civil wars and droughts. Beer is rarely available in the north, since Muslims do not consume alcohol. Chadians also enjoy cola, and some people make a type of fruit juice from the hibiscus plant, which they bottle at home. Everyone drinks tea sweetened with lots of sugar.

EATING HABITS

In Chad many people do not eat breakfast and those who do often simply eat leftovers from the day before. The main meal of the day is eaten at midday, and a smaller meal is eaten near sundown. Women usually do all the cooking over open fires. In many areas of Chad, women and children eat in a separate area from the men.

Chadians usually sit outdoors on mats to eat around a large common bowl. People will begin eating only after the host has prayed or indicated that everyone could start the meal. It is considered rude for a guest to refuse food, and when a guest stops eating, everyone else will also stop and consider their meal finished.

People do not like to eat in public as this is considered rude. To accommodate this, the interior of restaurants are hidden behind straw fences so that they cannot be seen from the street. Other conventions

A Chadian woman sells barrels of beer made from sorghum and millet.

A Chadian woman cooks a meal over an open fire.

concerning food include limiting what a pregnant woman may consume so that her baby will not be too big to deliver and refusing to give eggs to children lest they grow up to become thieves. Also, most people eat only with the right hand, which is a Muslim custom even non-Muslims follow.

For holidays, Chadians will eat a special stew called *marrara*. It is made from the intestines, stomach, liver, and kidneys of a goat and is considered a delicacy. In Chad, guests are always welcome, as hospitality is considered very important. A guest will always be offered refreshment, even if it is only a glass of water and a place to sit in the shade. If guests arrive near mealtime, they will be invited to join the family. If a person is going to be alone for a meal, he or she will either visit friends and family or invite someone else over. Eating is a communal activity in Chad and no one wants to eat alone. Women customarily prepare enough food for the family and a guest or two, just in case a friend or a neighbor drops by. No matter how little a family has, they will offer to share their food.

SQUASH WITH PEANUTS

2–3 pounds (1–1.3 kg) summer squash or zucchini
3 cups roasted peanuts (coarsely chopped or crushed)
2 tablespoons vegetable oil
1 teaspoon sugar
Salt

Boil the squash or zucchini in salted water until it becomes tender. Drain and mash. Add peanuts, fat, and sugar. Simmer the mixture over low heat until it becomes hot. Garnish with chopped peanuts. Serve hot.

KEFTA (SPICED MEATBALLS)

1 pound (0.5 kg) ground beef
1 tablespoon minced garlic
½ tablespoon ground cumin
2 tablespoons chopped parsley
1 bouillon cube
3 eggs
Salt and pepper to taste
Vegetable oil

Mix the meat, garlic, cumin, parsley, bouillon, salt, and pepper together. Boil eggs and quarter them. Mix them gradually into the meat mixture. Form the mixture into meatballs. Heat the cooking oil, and cook the meatballs for 10 to 15 minutes until the meat is fully cooked. Serve with salad or in a pita bread.

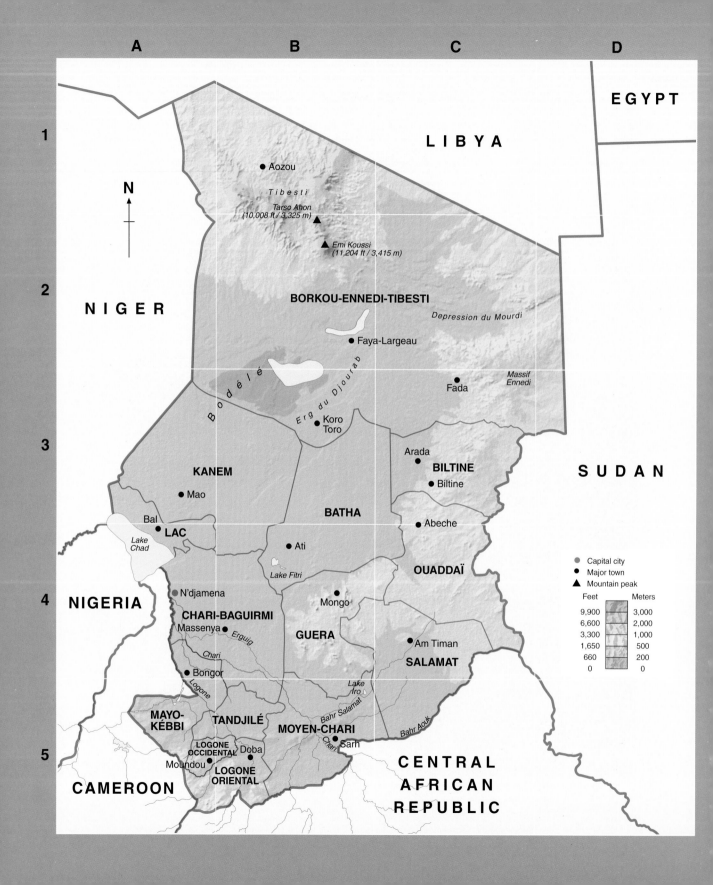

MAP OF CHAD

ECONOMIC CHAD

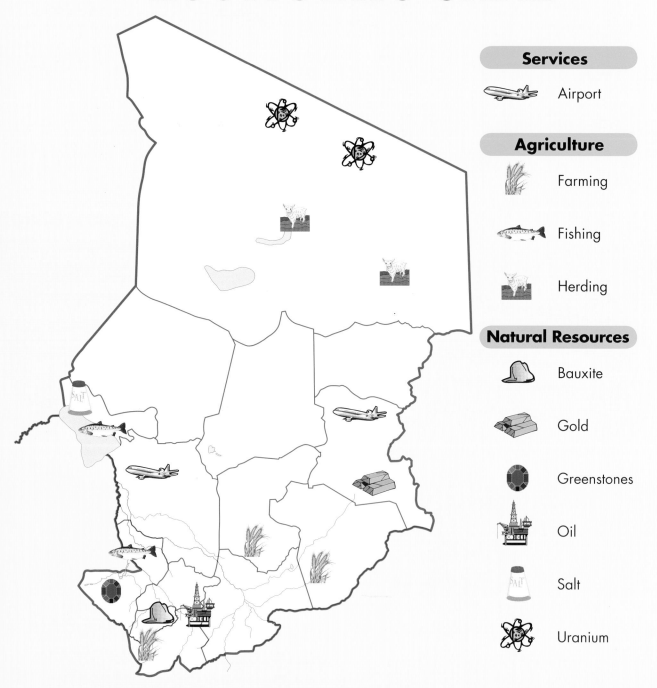

Services
✈ Airport

Agriculture
🌾 Farming

🐟 Fishing

🐐 Herding

Natural Resources
Bauxite

Gold

Greenstones

Oil

Salt

Uranium

ABOUT THE ECONOMY

GROSS DOMESTIC PRODUCT (GDP)
$10.67 billion (2004 estimate)

GDP BY SECTOR
Agriculture 32.4 percent, industry 18.8 percent, services 48.8 percent (2004 estimate)

POPULATION BELOW POVERTY LINE
80 percent (2001 estimate)

TOURISM
12,200 tourists per year

INFLATION
6 percent (2005 estimate)

WORKFORCE
More than 80 percent involved in subsistence farming or herding

CURRENCY
Communaute Financiere Africaine franc (XAF)—responsible authority is the Bank of the Central African States
U.S.$1 = 534.72 XAF (September 2005)
Denominations: Coins: 1, 5, 10, 25, 50, 100, 250 XAF; notes: 2,000

AGRICULTURAL PRODUCTS
Cotton, sorghum, millet, peanuts, rice, potatoes, cassava

MAJOR EXPORTS
Cotton, cattle, gum arabic

IMPORTS
Machinery, industrial goods, petroleum products, textiles, foodstuffs

MAJOR TRADING PARTNERS
France, United States, Cameroon, Netherlands

CULTURAL CHAD

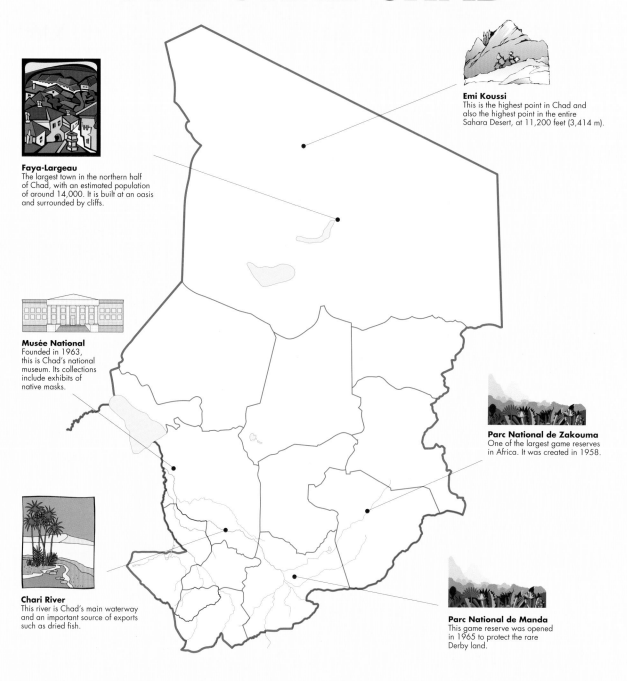

Emi Koussi
This is the highest point in Chad and also the highest point in the entire Sahara Desert, at 11,200 feet (3,414 m).

Faya-Largeau
The largest town in the northern half of Chad, with an estimated population of around 14,000. It is built at an oasis and surrounded by cliffs.

Musée National
Founded in 1963, this is Chad's national museum. Its collections include exhibits of native masks.

Parc National de Zakouma
One of the largest game reserves in Africa. It was created in 1958.

Chari River
This river is Chad's main waterway and an important source of exports such as dried fish.

Parc National de Manda
This game reserve was opened in 1965 to protect the rare Derby land.

ABOUT THE CULTURE

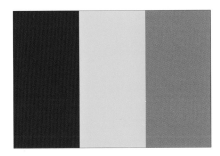

OFFICIAL NAME
Republic of Chad

FLAG
Three equal vertical bands with blue on the hoist side, then yellow and red. Design was based on the flag of France.

CAPITAL
N'Djamena

OTHER MAJOR CITIES
Moundou, Sarh, Abéché

POPULATION
9.8 million (2005 estimate)

ETHNIC GROUPS
More than 200 distinct groups. In the north: Arabs, Gorane, Zaghawa, Kanembou, Ouaddai, Baguirmi, Hadjerai, Fulani, Kotoko, Hausa, Boulala, Maba. In the south: Sara, Moundang, Moussei, Massa.

LIFE EXPECTANCY
48.2 years (2004 estimate)

MAJOR RELIGIONS
Muslim 51 percent, Christian 35 percent, animist 7 percent, other 7 percent

OFFICIAL LANGUAGES
French and Arabic

LITERACY RATE
47.5 percent

IMPORTANT ANNIVERSARY
Independence Day (August 11)

TIME LINE

IN CHAD	IN THE WORLD
	A.D. 600 Height of Mayan civilization
	1000 The Chinese perfect gunpowder and begin to use it in warfare.
	1530 Beginning of trans-Atlantic slave trade organized by the Portuguese in Africa.
1571–1603 Aluma is king of the Kanem-Borno kingdom in the region of Chad	**1558–1603** Reign of Elizabeth I of England
	1620 Pilgrims sail the *Mayflower* to America.
	1776 U.S. Declaration of Independence
	1789–99 The French Revolution
1808 The capital of the Kanem-Borno kingdom is ravaged by the Fulani.	**1861** The U.S. Civil War begins.
	1869 The Suez Canal is opened.
1900 Battle of Kousseri	**1914** World War I begins.
	1939 World War II begins.
	1945 The United States drops atomic bombs on Hiroshima and Nagasaki.
	1949 The North Atlantic Treaty Organization (NATO) is formed.
1959 The Republic of Chad is formed.	
1960 Proclamation of Chad's independence	
1962 One-party system is established in Chad.	**1966–69** The Chinese Cultural Revolution

IN CHAD	IN THE WORLD

1968
The Cultural Revolution plan is enacted.

1975
Francois Tombalbaye is assassinated.

1978
Hissen Habré becomes Chad's premier.

1980
Civil war breaks out. Almost all of N'Djamena's inhabitants flee to Cameroon.

1984
France and Libya agree on the terms of Libyan withdrawal from Chad.

1986
Nuclear power disaster at Chernobyl in Ukraine

1989
Chad–Libya peace accord is signed.

1990
Idriss Deby becomes the president of Chad.

1991
Break-up of the Soviet Union

1994
The International Court of Justice in The Hague confirms that Chad, not Libya, has sovereignty over the Aouzou strip. Libyan troops leave the Aouzou strip.

1996
Idriss Deby wins the presidental election.

1997
Hong Kong is returned to China.

2001
Idriss Deby is re-elected president.

2001
Terrorists crash planes in New York, Washington, D.C., and Pennsylvania.

2003
War in Iraq

2004
Chad receives the first oil payments from the Chad–Cameroon pipeline project.

2006
Idriss Deby wins the presidential election.

GLOSSARY

bili-bili
Homemade beer made by women using millet.

boule
The staple food of Chad, usually made of millet.

gon lere
Traditional leader of the Moundang.

groundnuts
Peanuts

hajj
The pilgrimage to Mecca that all Muslims should make at least once in their lives if they can afford it.

marrara
A special holiday meal made from the internal organs of a goat.

margai
Spirits worshiped by the Hadjeray.

bang
The title of the leader of the Baguirmi kingdom. Also, a chief of the Sara people.

nashif
A spicy northern sauce that contains beef.

noi
A caste among the Sara who perform priestly functions.

polders
A series of dikes and periodically flooded fields along the northern end of Lake Chad.

razzias
Slave-raiding parties of the past, outlawed by the French.

yondo
A Sara initiation rite for young men that was revived during Tombalbaye's cultural revolution.

FURTHER INFORMATION

BOOKS

Azevedo, Mario J. and Emmanuel U. Nnadozie. *Chad: A Nation in Search of its Future.* Boulder, CO: Westview Press, 1998.

Collelo, Thomas, ed. *Chad, a Country Study.* Headquarters, Department of the Army, United States Government, 1990.

Riesman, Paul. *Freedom in Fulani Social Life.* Chicago: University of Chicago Press, 1977.

WEB SITES

Central Intelligence Agency World Factbook. (Select Chad from country list) www.cia.gov/cia/publications/factbook/index.html

Chad-Society Index. www.photius.com/countries/chad/society/index.html

Human Rights Watch: Chad. www.hrw.org/doc?t=africa&c=chad

Lonely Planet World Guide: Destination Chad. www.lonelyplanet.com/destinations/africa/chad/

FILMS

Bye, Bye Africa. California Newsreel, 1999.

Daresalam. Kino International, 2005.

People and Places of Africa: Chad. Powersports Productions, 1998.

BIBLIOGRAPHY

Dalby, Andrew. *Dictionary of Languages*. New York: Columbia University Press, 2004.

Mays, Terry M. *Africa's First Peacekeeping Operation: The OAU in Chad*, 1981–1982. Westport, Connecticut: Praeger Publishers, 2002.

Riesman, Paul. *Freedom in Fulani Social Life*. Chicago: University of Chicago Press, 1977.

CIES.org. "Chad." www.cies.org/country/chad.htm

CNN.com. "Africa's Great Shrinking Lake Chad." http://archives.cnn.com/2001/TECH/science/02/27/shrinking.lakechad/

CNN.com. "Fossils Make Case for Apparent Human Ancestor." www.cnn.com/2005/TECH/science/04/06/human.ancestor.ap/index.html

Infoplease.com. "Chad." www.infoplease.com/ipa/A0107403.html

International Campaign to Ban Landmines. "Chad." www.icbl.org/lm/2000/chad.html

Mbendi.co.za. "Chad: Mining Overview." www.mbendi.co.za/indy/ming/af/ch/p0005.htm

Photius.com. "Chad Sara: Sedentary Peoples of the Soudanian Zone." www.photius.com/countries/chad/society/chad_society_sara_sedentary_peop~826.html

INDEX